THE HOLDUP

by
MARSHA NORMAN

**DRAMATISTS
PLAY SERVICE
INC.**

THE HOLDUP
Copyright © 1987, Marsha Norman

All Rights Reserved

CAUTION: Professionals and amateurs are hereby warned that performance of THE HOLDUP is subject to a royalty. It is fully protected under the copyright laws of the United States of America, and of all countries covered by the International Copyright Union (including the Dominion of Canada and the rest of the British Commonwealth), and of all countries covered by the Pan-American Copyright Convention, the Universal Copyright Convention, the Berne Convention, and of all countries with which the United States has reciprocal copyright relations. All rights, including professional/amateur stage rights, motion picture, recitation, lecturing, public reading, radio broadcasting, television, video or sound recording, all other forms of mechanical or electronic reproduction, such as CD-ROM, CD-I, information storage and retrieval systems and photocopying, and the rights of translation into foreign languages, are strictly reserved. Particular emphasis is laid upon the matter of readings, permission for which must be secured from the Author's agent in writing.

The stage performance rights in THE HOLDUP (other than first class rights) are controlled exclusively by the DRAMATISTS PLAY SERVICE, INC., 440 Park Avenue South, New York, N.Y. 10016. No professional or non-professional performance of the Play (excluding first class professional performance) may be given without obtaining in advance the written permission of the DRAMATISTS PLAY SERVICE, INC., and paying the requisite fee.

Inquiries concerning all other rights should be addressed to Jack Tantleff c/o The Tantleff Office, 375 Greenwich Street, Suite 700, New York, N.Y. 10013.

SPECIAL NOTE

Anyone receiving permission to produce THE HOLDUP is required to give credit to the Author as sole and exclusive Author of the Play on the title page of all programs distributed in connection with performances of the Play and in all instances in which the title of the Play appears for purposes of advertising, publicizing or otherwise exploiting the Play and/or a production thereof. The name of the Author must appear on a separate line, in which no other name appears, immediately beneath the title and in size of type equal to 50% of the largest, most prominent letter used for the title of the Play. No person, firm or entity may receive credit larger or more prominent than that accorded the Author.

THE HOLDUP was presented at the American Conservatory Theatre in San Francisco on April 12, 1983. It was directed by Edward Hastings; the scenery was by Richard Seger; the costumes were by Michael Casey; the lighting was by Robert Peterson; the assistant director was Michael Pulizzano. The cast was as follows:

THE OUTLAW........................... Peter Donat

ARCHIE TUCKER....................... Tom O'Brien

HENRY TUCKER..................... Lawrence Hecht

LILY................................ Barbara Dirickson

CAST

THE OUTLAW — A worn, grizzled desperado, now approaching 50. He is fearless and mean-tempered, a wily survivor of the Hole-in-the-Wall era, who never says more than is necessary and who generally gets what he wants because he knows how to stand there and mean business.

LILY — A frontier beauty, a little past her prime. She has graciously accepted the wisdom and perspective that have replaced her once startling appearance. In the old days, she was a dance hall favorite. Now, she owns the finest hotel east of Albuquerque.

ARCHIE TUCKER — A green Clovis boy of 17. Archie's open face and simple enthusiasm seem quite out of place in this barren country. He talks too much and smiles too much and complains too much and all in all, doesn't belong here. He's eager to find a way out but is held back by his mother and his age and his fear, in general.

HENRY TUCKER — Archie's hothead rancher brother. Henry is mean and tough, a foul-mouthed, heavy drinking cattleman, a bit embarrassed to be supplementing his income by working this wheat threshing crew. He is 30 years old but still lives at home. His youth was baked dry in the sun of too many days doing his endless, lifeless work. His sole entertainment is reading outlaw books. He is an expert in their methods and manners.

The play takes place around a cookshack belonging to a wheat threshing crew working a field in northern New Mexico in the fall of 1914. It is miles from nowhere and long past sundown.

THE HOLDUP

ACT I

Night in New Mexico is dark and flat. And if you are alone, you are always lost, even if you think you know where you are going.

There are two strays in this night, headed straight for each other, but they don't know that. We see their faces but we don't know where they are. We only know that they are alone, and they are dealing with their respective problems as best they can, determined to reach what they think is a safe place, the company of other humans.

The Outlaw takes his saddle off the horse and ties up the cinches so he can carry it. And he talks.

OUTLAW. Well, old girl, I've shot better horses than you, but never one I felt so kin to, at the moment. *(And now, from another part of the blackness comes a terrified voice, a shaky praying voice.)*
ARCHIE. Jesus God in Heaven, it's Archie Tucker from Clovis, New Mexico. I know you can see me, so I know you can see that coyote that's following me and I don't know if he's alone, but I'm alone and I need you to keep him back there 'til I can run for the cookshack, which shouldn't be too much longer, now, thank you so much, Amen.
OUTLAW. *(Taking off the bridle.)* I just don't have any choice about shootin' you, see. I can't just leave you here to die by *yourself.* And I can't hobble along with you or I'll miss Lily. I told her I'd be there at midnight, sharp. Nice and easy, girl, here it comes. *(And we hear the gunshot, and Archie hears it, too, but he has other concerns.)*

ARCHIE. Uh, Lord, you gave me a gun, I know, but Henry, that's my brother, he's got it standing guard back at the cookshack. So it's just you and me and that coyote. I'd stand and fight him but I imagine I'd die, if you know what I mean. People die out here all the time and nobody ever knows. Tell you what, I'll run when I can.

OUTLAW. You know who I miss? That gelding. Suzy. Snaggletooth horse. She was! Who am I talking to. Just pick up your gear and walk, old man. Just another mile, buddy. Lily always had an eye for horseflesh, didn't she? She'll bring you somethin sweet to ride, you can count on that, at least. *(And we hear him begin to walk.)*

ARCHIE. Uh, Lord, in case you saw me ride into town today, maybe you got me mixed up with the rest of the boys stayed in town to ... all right, but I don't like to even *say* it. They stayed in town to drink beer and abuse women. I am *not* one of them, I am *saved* and I need some help here. Oh boy. I bet you hear that a lot. Well, listen, forget about everybody else for a while. This is serious.

OUTLAW. Well what have we got up here? Looks like some kind of cookshack, some wheat threshing crew I guess. Well sure, it is. It's the water hole, isn't it? Only water for twenty miles, as I remember. Think she's here yet? Think she's as old as you are? Think she's gonna show up at all? What do you do if she don't, huh?

ARCHIE. *(His voice showing his relief.)* Oh now, there's the cookshack, I can just about make it now. Thank you so much. Run, Archie!

OUTLAW. *(Hearing Archie screaming.)* What the hell? *(And now we see the cookshack and the barrels and benches that huddle around it. It is a small wood building on wheels with one door, one window and a metal chimney for ventilation. There are heavy cloth flaps hanging down to the ground on all sides protecting the sleeping area underneath it. You wonder how it continues to stand up, but you have no doubt that it does. There are some curiously modern-looking machine parts lying around, but otherwise, the scene looks almost pre-Civil War. And Archie comes*

barreling onto the stage, terrified.)
ARCHIE. Henry! Hey in there, Henry Tucker! *(Banging on the cookshack door.)* You gotta hear what just happened to me when I'm coming back from town just now. *(Jumps up to the window, trying to wake Henry.)* Henry! Wake up! I know you're in there, Henry, and you know who this is so you open this door, Henry. *(Still no answer.)* Did you know they were gonna stay in town all night? Get cleaned up, that's what they said. But then... *(Screaming.)* Henry! *(And the door finally opens.)* Nobody acts right out here. I hate this place!
HENRY. So leave, priss, the train runs both ways, Archie.
ARCHIE. You're not gonna believe what happened, Henry!
HENRY. *(Starting to build the fire back up, not eager to hear anything.)* It won't be worth wakin' up for, I can tell that already.
ARCHIE. I jumped off the train, only right away I'm not alone, see. I turn around and there he was, standing sideways in the road, the biggest coyote I ever saw. So I started up walking again, but when I speeded up, he speeded up and when I slowed down, he slowed down and finally, I got where I could see the cookshack and took off running and here I am.
HENRY. And that's your big story?
ARCHIE. I mean, I could hardly breathe there for a while.
HENRY. You ran away? Damn right it's your big story. Got a problem? Call Henry or run away. Runt coward. You make me sick, Archie. I don't know what I was doing, bringing you along. Dad's probably still laughing at me stuck out here with you.
ARCHIE. I've got as much right to be here as you do. They hired us both. Mr. White says I'm a good worker.
HENRY. They hired you because they couldn't get me unless they took you. What do you know about threshing wheat, Archie? They all laugh at you, you know. You're a joke, Archie.
ARCHIE. Well just how hard do you think the boys would laugh if they saw your pillow full of outlaw books, huh? Every spare minute you get, sneaking off to ride with the Wild Bunch, fighting the Johnson County War.
HENRY. The Wild Bunch didn't fight the Johnson County War.

ARCHIE. Well who cares whether they did or they didn't? That stuff is made up, Henry. People write those books just to find out if anybody's dumb enough to believe it.

HENRY. Bout like the Bible, I guess.

ARCHIE. The Bible is the truth.

HENRY. People walk out on the water and get swallowed by whales, Archie?

ARCHIE. It has to be the truth, Henry. What do you think God's trying to do, entertain?

HENRY. Just leave me alone, O.K. Just go to bed, Diddly.

ARCHIE. Don't call me that!

HENRY. Just don't say one more word to me, you think you can do that? I get rid of you for one night in my whole life and what do you do? Take the train right on back here.

ARCHIE. You're just mad about Corbin in town spendin all your pay you gambled off last night. It serves you right, pulling your gun like one of your outlaws, for God's sake. I hope you learned your lesson.

HENRY. They've had it in for me since the beginning of this job, Archie. I don't know who they think they are, these cowboys, they're just as dumb and just as worn out as everybody else I know. Bunch of sheepherders, if you ask me. So I showed em, that's all. Now, you just watch and see if anybody ever tries to cheat Henry Tucker again. What do I want to go into town for anyway? Have a good time with that bunch of know-it-alls? Fat chance.

ARCHIE. Oh I almost forgot! Guess what else I saw in town? Marines signing up men for the war. It's all over the papers too. Some Archduke Somebody-or-other got killed and it's all about to blow up!

HENRY. *(Not the least bit interested.)* What is?

ARCHIE. The world, Henry! Unless we get there in time!

HENRY. So why didn't you join up?

ARCHIE. Mother would *kill* me!

HENRY. So would a war, Archie.

ARCHIE. You could go! You're exactly who they're lookin' for! They're gonna fly airplanes in this war, Henry! You'd like that, zoomin around the sky. You could be The Outlaw of the Air, Henry!

HENRY. Well, they better not take you, Archie. You'd be out there on the front lines, walk over to the enemy and say, "Hi there, my name is Archie and these are my buddies, this is Ralph and this is Joey and we're from New Mexico" and you'd be the first Marine who ever died in the middle of a sentence. *(Archie turns away.)* What's the matter with you? Guys like us go to war and we don't get to fly airplanes. We just stand on the ground and get shot. Don't make any sense at all, Archie. I can do that here.

ARCHIE. He told me I could learn to fly a plane. I asked him and he said, "Come on."

HENRY. Just shut up. You don't know what you're talking about.

ARCHIE. O.K. O.K. *(And then, in a moment of silence, they hear a twig break just behind the cookshack. Whispering.)* What was that?

HENRY. *(Covering his fear.)* Well, it sure as hell ain't the Marines. *(Henry picks up a stick of wood from the fire and Archie backs away, toward Henry for protection, and the Outlaw appears, gun raised, from the other direction, surprising them both. The Outlaw looks quite different than when we saw him before. Maybe it's the effect of the gun in his hand. Maybe he likes horses better than people. Whatever it is, this is somebody you don't want to fool around with. This man looks dangerous.)*

OUTLAW. Keep on talking, boy. *(Waving the pistol at Henry.)* Hands high, cowboy. *(Archie raises his hands.)* Not you, boy. You sit. Over there. Him. Up.

ARCHIE. *(As Henry is reluctant.)* Henry!

OUTLAW. That's better. Don't need any heroes here. Just a little hospitality.

HENRY. *(As the Outlaw searches him.)* What do you want, gramps?

OUTLAW. *(Not easing the tension one bit.)* Oh, I don't know. What have you got?

ARCHIE. Anything you want. You just name it.

HENRY. *(Turning quickly.)* Shut up, Archie.

OUTLAW. *(Poking Henry with the gun, not liking that fast turn.)* Careful, cowboy.

ARCHIE. His name's Henry.

HENRY. Shut up, Archie! *(Then quickly.)* How long have you been out there?

OUTLAW. *(Still very threatening.)* Long enough. You don't look a thing alike.

ARCHIE. He takes after Dad. That whole side of the family is...

HENRY. Shut up, Archie. The man's not here to get a family history. What do you want, mister?

OUTLAW. Eggs. Cooked.

HENRY. No.

ARCHIE. I'll make em, Henry, if you want me to.

HENRY. I said No.

OUTLAW. Yes. And if you got a gun in the cookshack, there, you just bring it right on out here.

HENRY. Maybe I will.

OUTLAW. Yeah, you go get it and then you'll draw on me and I'll kill you. Won't be anything personal, just how it happens to me anymore. I get what I want. Now, I want some eggs.

HENRY. Any man can walk in hungry and ask for eggs and I'll make em, any day, but you ain't asked.

OUTLAW. Are we gonna fight over a mess of eggs?

ARCHIE. *(Trying to be reasonable.)* I said I'd make the eggs. The man's a stranger here and we should...

HENRY. *(Stops him, rough.)* Don't you move. You do what I say.

ARCHIE. Then you do what he says.

HENRY. Don't tell me what to do!

ARCHIE. I'm not. What do I know? It's just ... you do see the gun, don't you, Henry? We're just talking about some old eggs, Henry.

OUTLAW. Don't you want to get your gun?

HENRY. I'll cook. *(And Henry heads for the cookshack.)*

OUTLAW. And bring me some whiskey.

ARCHIE. We don't have any whiskey. We got a rule about it.
OUTLAW. If you didn't have any whiskey, you wouldn't have a rule about it. *(And now, the Outlaw walks behind the water barrels to retrieve his saddle over a bale of hay to make a kind of seat, but he doesn't sit on it. Archie watches as long as he can before he talks.)*
ARCHIE. Are you gonna kill us?
OUTLAW. I'm gonna eat first.
ARCHIE. That's not fair! We're minding our own business. It's Saturday night. We threshed wheat all week, we work hard. Then we get a night off and you come up and shoot us. It's not fair. It's not civilized. We're a state now. It's 1914.
OUTLAW. Do you know what a joke is? You know, one person says a funny thing to some other person and the other person laughs? *(No response.)* Do you? Joke? Ha-ha?
ARCHIE. I know that.
OUTLAW. Then why didn't you laugh at my joke?
ARCHIE. Are you gonna kill us or not?
OUTLAW. Are you always like this? *(No response.)* What time is it?
ARCHIE. Oh, you're meeting somebody here! What a good idea. It's a perfect place for it. Why didn't you say that in the first place. Maybe we've seen em already. Nope. Nobody for hours, now, well, what do I know? I just got back myself. Maybe Henry saw somebody. Who're we lookin for? Tall? Thin?
OUTLAW. I just asked you what time it was.
ARCHIE. Oh. Right. I don't know. Dark.
OUTLAW. What does Henry do? How come he's out here with everyday else on the town for the night?
ARCHIE. The crew could come back any time, you know. There's twenty-five or more. Big men.
OUTLAW. *(Screaming.)* I want those eggs, cowboy! *(Then normally.)* They call you Archie?
ARCHIE. Or Doc. Some of em call me Doc. *(The Outlaw nods, but doesn't ask why.)* I was sweet on Doc Porter's girl, Sarah. They started calling me Doc because, well, Doc Porter runs the drugstore in Clovis. I'm courting a Doc's daughter so they call me Doc. It's a joke.

OUTLAW. It isn't very funny for a joke.

ARCHIE. Or fork-pitcher. It's what I do. I fork up the wheat and

OUTLAW. *(Interrupting.)* pitch it on the wagon, I know. What's that big machine out there?

ARCHIE. It's a brand new separator. Thing threshes ten times as much wheat as the old one in half the time. Gonna change everything.

OUTLAW. It takes up too much room. It's ugly. *(Henry comes out of the cookshack carrying a steaming plate of eggs, and now wearing a light jacket.)*

HENRY. *(Heartily, as though he'd cooked for a friend.)* Six eggs. Hot and ready!

ARCHIE. I told you he'd make the eggs.

OUTLAW. *(Referring to the coat.)* Got you gun, I see.

HENRY. Cold out here. Eat up. That's a clean fork.

OUTLAW. *(Walking toward Archie, picking up a forkful of eggs.)* I was asking Archie, how come you pulled this guard duty while the rest of the boys are in raisin' hell tonight. *(He pushes the bite of eggs in Archie's mouth.)*

HENRY. Somebody has to.

OUTLAW. Yeah, but why you, cowboy? What happened last night?

HENRY. It's none of your business.

OUTLAW. Oh yes it is, too. I want to hear it. Archie will tell me, won't you boy? Eggs taste good, cowboy.

HENRY. *(To Archie.)* You do and I'll...

OUTLAW. *(Demanding.)* Archie!

ARCHIE. *(Beginning rather helplessly.)* It was just another stupid poker game. Corbin was cheating and I saw it. I told Henry and Henry drew on him. That's all.

OUTLAW. If that was all, Archie, Mr. Corbin would be out here eatin' hay, not Henry.

HENRY. *(Before Archie can start.)* You shut your mouth, priss.

ARCHIE. *(As the Outlaw plays with his gun, just to terrify Archie.)* The gun is why Henry's out here. Not supposed to have guns in

camp, that's all.
OUTLAW. *(Not satisfied.)* Go on.
ARCHIE. *(Compulsively.)* All right! When Henry drew his gun he dropped his cards and there's not supposed to be two ace of hearts either! *(The Outlaw laughs and now Archie can't stop talking.)* They woulda killed each other if Mr. White hadn't been here. They woulda both lost their jobs, too, if this wasn't twenty square miles of wheat to thresh next week. They were acting like some saloon characters from twenty years ago.
OUTLAW. Man's got to protect himself, Archie.
ARCHIE. Yeah, but he's supposed to use his brain, not his gun.
OUTLAW. Well, you want to use the quickest thing you got, whatever that is.
ARCHIE. You shouldn't cheat til you learn how to play, Henry.
HENRY. You started it all, Archie. I'd be spendin' his money right now if it wasn't for you and your big mouth. "Corbin's cheatin, Henry," like a damn idiot.
OUTLAW. Henry's right, Archie. You talk too much.
HENRY. There's a horse comin'.
OUTLAW. *(Quite calm, having heard it already.)* Uh-huh.
HENRY. *(Nodding in agreement.)* Sounds like a Morgan horse to me.
OUTLAW. *(Watching Archie, playing along.)* Black, with ... white feet.
HENRY. Seven, eight years old maybe.
OUTLAW. *(Knows it isn't a horse, by now.)* Still got all his teeth, though. *(And they laugh and Archie was completely taken in.)*
ARCHIE. It's the rest of your gang, I guess. *(Then quite dispirited, to Henry.)* He asked me while ago what time it was, Henry.
HENRY. Relax, Archie. It's just Mother comin' to collect you for prayer meeting.
ARCHIE. I hear it now. It doesn't sound like a horse at all. It sounds like an automobile! *(They laugh.)* It does!
HENRY. Archie, the closest road is five miles from here.

OUTLAW. *(Very concerned by now.)* So if it is a car, it's a damn fool drivin' it.
ARCHIE. *(Feeling quite anxious.)* How did *you* get here? Where's your horse?
OUTLAW. Bout a mile back.
ARCHIE. I could get him for you.
OUTLAW. You could have her for breakfast.
ARCHIE. She's dead.
OUTLAW. I shot her.
ARCHIE. You saw the fire and walked to here.
OUTLAW. Oh there's no foolin' you, is there, Archie?
ARCHIE. *(Staring out into the night.)* It sure is a car all right. Are they lost or what? Who'd come out here in a car? *(Then as Henry and the Outlaw are both very anxious, and clearly not willing to speculate about who this might be in the car, Archie goes on babbling.)* Was she a good horse?
HENRY. Would you shoot a good horse, Archie? Yes, you would. Archie would shoot a good horse if Mother told him to.
ARCHIE. Good horses get sick.
HENRY. *(Testing the Outlaw.)* A man shoots his horse is shootin' off his pecker, Archie.
OUTLAW. Shut up, cowboy.
HENRY. I was saying not to ask about it. It ain't your business, Archie. It makes you feel bad to shoot your horse. As bad as *(Turning around to face the Outlaw.)* shootin' off your pecker so don't make jokes about it.
ARCHIE. I wasn't joking, I was asking.
OUTLAW. *(As the car stops.)* Archie don't use his pecker anyway, so he wouldn't know.
ARCHIE. I do too. Use it. *(Henry and the Outlaw laugh.)* I water the garden. *(They laugh and he continues.)* I put out fires. *(More laughter.)* Cuts the dust right off a wagon wheel.
OUTLAW. *(Getting his gun out again.)* Go on.
ARCHIE. That's all.
OUTLAW. *(Covering his nervousness about who's coming.)* You just been doin' chores with it? You ain't had any fun with it?

ARCHIE. Leave me alone.
OUTLAW. Any girls took a peek at it?
HENRY. Hell, he doesn't even look at it.
ARCHIE. Who's side are you on, Henry? *(And now, from offstage, we hear a voice full of anticipation.)*
LILY. Tom? Tom?
HENRY. What is this?
OUTLAW. Sounds like a lady came in a car.
ARCHIE. Tom? Is that your name, Tom? *(And Lily rushes onstage, wearing a Barney Oldfield-type duster over her long split riding skirt. It all looks very expensive, but is clearly western and meant for hard use.*
LILY. Tom!
OUTLAW. *(Reacting to the duster.)* What the hell?
LILY. *(Thrilled to see him, but stops herself from running to him once she sees Archie and Henry.)* You are! You're still alive!
OUTLAW. *(Concealing whatever he feels.)* Well I wouldn't write you to tell you I was dead!
LILY. But anybody could've written that letter. Your handwriting's not as...
OUTLAW. *(Interrupting.)* Take that thing off. Let me look at you.
LILY. *(Delighted to.)* Just a minute. I almost didn't find this place, you know. They cut down that cottonwood tree. Good thing the water hole's still here. *(The jacket is off now.)* Now!
OUTLAW. Oh that's much better. You haven't changed a bit.
LILY. *(Walking into his arms.)* It's going to work out just fine, isn't it? I'm getting old and you're going blind. *(And he turns her around to them, not able to give her quite the greeting he wanted to, but still obviously desperate to touch her.)*
ARCHIE. Did you really come all the way out here in a car?
LILY. Big black Buick. Go see for yourself! *(Archie starts off toward the car, but Henry stops him.)*
OUTLAW. Lily, this is the Tucker Brothers. Archie and Cowboy.
ARCHIE. His name's Henry.

OUTLAW. Boys, meet Lily.

LILY. *(She nods to them, but talks to the Outlaw.)* What a ride! That's at least forty miles! And there's no road at all for the last five!

OUTLAW. *(Starting for the bench now.)* Well, here, why don't you sit down a minute and...

HENRY. *(Disgusted.)* Look, folks. This ain't exactly Main Street out here. Could you take your visit on down the road so we can get some sleep?

OUTLAW. *(Ignoring Henry and walking her to the bench.)* There's no road, remember?

LILY. Boy, we're in big trouble if we have a blowout out here, I guess I could have rented a horse, but, oh, Tom, *(In a mock scolding.)* Where have you been?

HENRY. *(Irritated, but beginning to be curious.)* How come he couldn't meet you in town? Been a helluva lot easier to find.

OUTLAW. *(Breaking away from Lily.)* Can you shut your mouth and do whatever I tell you to do? Can you get the lady a drink and not ask any stupid questions, cowboy? *(Henry doesn't move.)* And I told you while ago I wanted some whiskey but I don't see it out here, now, do I? Move!

HENRY. One drink and you go?

OUTLAW. Get it. *(And Henry goes into the cookshack and the Outlaw turns back to Lily.)* Why the hell did you buy an automobile?

LILY. For the horn. I like the horn. A little man brought it. I kept him too. He ... works on it.

ARCHIE. That's where I saw you! Outside that fancy hotel in town.

LILY. Oh Tom, you wouldn't know the old place now. It's solid white paint, no wallpaper. There's actually trees growing in barrels all along that front hall. Oh and the dining room is this bright green and Roy Luther hooked me up a waterfall, inside the dining room. And I'm about ready to go order another automobile to pick up my guests at the train station. They come in hot and thirsty and see those trees and that waterfall and they feel like staying a *week*.

ARCHIE. I saw that car too. That's some car all right.
OUTLAW. You think she's pretty?
ARCHIE. She's pretty.
OUTLAW. You got any money?
ARCHIE. I worked hard for it, if I do, and I'm not handing it over, no sir.
OUTLAW. Money for the lady. How much you got?
ARCHIE. I'm not interested in that.
LILY. And the price has gone way up, mister.
OUTLAW. You squirmy little mole. Tell me how much money you got!
ARCHIE. Twenty-eight dollars.
OUTLAW. You could have this pretty lady, all day, all night for a solid month with that money. All to yourself, just you and her. You ever thought about that?
ARCHIE. No.
OUTLAW. *(As Henry comes out with the whiskey.)* Do you know what you're going to be when you grow up?
ARCHIE. No.
OUTLAW. Sorry, that's what. *(And the Outlaw and Henry have a good laugh about that.)*
LILY. Do you know what year this is? I'm not a whore. It's not a whorehouse. It's a hotel now and I own it.
OUTLAW. *(Clearly annoyed.)* A little pride goes a long way, girl.
LILY. I *told* them you were still alive. I just *knew* it. Roy Luther said Bob Ford got you.
HENRY. Bob Ford got Jesse James.
LILY. Daisy said it was Frank Canton.
HENRY. *(More energy than we've seen from him all night.)* He got Nate Champion at the Johnson County War.
LILY. Gus figured it was the Pinkertons. Chase you down like Kid Curry.
HENRY. Kid Curry killed himself.
OUTLAW. And I bet you know where.
HENRY. I do, that's true. Parachute, Colorado.

ARCHIE. Henry believes in outlaws.
HENRY. Shut up, Archie.
LILY. *(Laughs.)* Roy Luther swore he saw it in the papers.
OUTLAW. He saw Bill and Fred. They got Bill and Fred.
HENRY. Bill Carver?
OUTLAW. Bill my brother. His boy Fred. Nice boy, big hands.
LILY. Guess he just saw the name then.
HENRY. What name?
OUTLAW. *(Ignoring Henry.)* Well, how do I look? Old?
HENRY. Hey, your eggs got cold before you finished them. How 'bout some more eggs.
OUTLAW. We aren't gonna be here long enough for that, cowboy.
HENRY. Sure you are. The lady's tired and you could use some more food, pops. It looks like it's been a while. You want anything, ma'am? Might be a corn stick left from supper.
LILY. No thank you.
HENRY. Well, you just let me know if you change your mind. And just take your time there. We're glad to have you. Gets awful lonely out here.
ARCHIE. *(Dumfounded but pleased by this change in Henry.)* See how nice Henry can be when he wants to?
LILY. Have you seen Bub Meeks?
OUTLAW. Lost a leg in prison, last I heard.
HENRY. They shot him trying to escape. Climbing up the walls at Idaho Federal.
OUTLAW. Well you're a real outlaw expert, aren't you, cowboy?
HENRY. Want your eggs sunny-side up, this time?
OUTLAW. *(Now eager to get rid of him.)* That sounds good.
HENRY. Comin' right up.
LILY. *(As Henry goes into the cookshack.)* Anybody else?
OUTLAW. They're in Bolivia, you know. Butch is alive.
ARCHIE. That's in South America.
OUTLAW. Thank you.

ARCHIE. I go to school.
OUTLAW. Or dead. Boliva or dead.
ARCHIE. I don't get it.
OUTLAW. I wasn't talking to you.
ARCHIE. Your folks, is that it?
OUTLAW. Yeah, boy. My folks all died.
ARCHIE. Or went to Bolivia.
OUTLAW. *(Ignoring Archie.)* I've got a new picture with me. I want you to take it to the Western Union and switch it. Burn that one from Telluride.
LILY. I always thought it was better of Butch than you.
OUTLAW. This is a much better picture.
LILY. I had my picture made for my birthday. Beside my Buick. In front of my hotel. Wearing my duster and goggles. Looks like I cut it out of a magazine but it's me all right.
ARCHIE. Are we talking about a wanted poster?
OUTLAW. *We* were.
LILY. Well actually, *he* was.
ARCHIE. You want them to catch you?
OUTLAW. No, I don't want them to catch me. But I do want them to know what I look like now. I got my pride. *(To Lily.)* You're prettier than you were.
LILY. It's the money. Are you going to Bolivia?
OUTLAW. It's a long trip, but I bet they'd make you the goddamn queen of Bolivia.
ARCHIE. Do you speak Spanish? They speak Spanish.
OUTLAW. *(Furious with him.)* If I want to go to Bolivia, I'll go to Bolivia. They have tin mines there. Did you learn that in school? I'll rob mine payrolls. And I'll eat those green bananas and I'll lay around with this lady and have our dinner cooked by some mountain kid about your age who knows not to say a goddamned thing like who are you or what do you want. Except he will say Good Morning and Thank you, Muchas gracias. And we'll have a wonderful time and we won't think about you or all the people like you back here building houses and running for mayor.
ARCHIE. This is the best country in the world! I could be president!

OUTLAW. That's why we're talking about Bolivia! What's the matter with you?

LILY. You can't go to Bolivia either. The trip alone would kill you. And how do you know you *like* bananas?

OUTLAW. Don't you want to see the lady's car, boy? *(And Archie gets out of there quickly, knowing they want to be alone.)* Got a kiss for the old man? *(They kiss and we see him relax for just a moment.)*

LILY. *(Tenderly.)* You look awfully tired, Tom. I heard you were working horses in Montana, but you look like you've been living in a cave.

OUTLAW. *(A sense of purpose now.)* I've been ... seeing your face.

LILY. This face? Or the old one. The young one?

OUTLAW. I mean ... I think about you.

LILY. I waited for you to come back, you know. I kept eggs in the house for two years for you.

OUTLAW. Well, here I am, girl.

LILY. *(She has a small laugh.)* So I see.

OUTLAW. *(Impatient as always.)* You know what I want. Yes or no?

LILY. Yes or no what? I've seen you one day in the last twenty years!

OUTLAW. Helluva day.

LILY. What do you want, Tom?

OUTLAW. *(Her directness backs him off.)* Well, like I said in my letter, I ... *(The more he looks at her, the more he can't say what he's come all these miles to say.)* I had some business down this way.

LILY. What business? Twenty years is a long time. Things happen. Tell me what your business is. Tell me what you want me to say yes or no to. Then ask me. A girl needs to hear a man talk a little.

OUTLAW. About what?

LILY. No, don't say anything now. I'm rested enough, I think. Come back to town with me. You'll be safe enough. They all think you're dead anyway. And if anybody asks who you are, which they won't, I'll say you're my father. *(He backs off even further.)* I'll get

you whatever you want to eat and you can stay as long as you like. You'll like the hotel, there's lots of fancy eastern folks coming through all the time and we're getting our telephone next month so...
OUTLAW. *(Interrupting.)* What ever happened to your rancher friend?
LILY. You shot him.
OUTLAW. Oh that's right I did.
LILY. *(Trying to regain his attention.)* He died. Tom. Roy Luther is dying to see you. It'll be just like you remember. You'll get a bath and some sleep and you can tell me everything you've done for the last...
OUTLAW. You want to hear me *talk?*
LILY. I want to know if you're still the man I knew, that's all.
OUTLAW. Well, the girl I knew...
LILY. Is right here, Tom.
OUTLAW. Woulda brought me a horse. *(And the Outlaw stands up now, and Henry opens the cookshack door and Archie returns looking at the car.)*
ARCHIE. *(Running up to Henry, a conspiratorial tone in his voice.)* He's an outlaw, Henry. They've got his picture at the Western Union.
HENRY. He's no outlaw, Archie. Just some old prospector lost track of the mother lode, huh, pops? You were pannin' for gold and you lost your pan. Well, we got plenty more inside. Take this one when you're through with the eggs.
ARCHIE. Henry, he's with Butch Cassidy in this picture. They're at Telluride in this picture.
HENRY. *(Appreciating the clue.)* Is that so? Well, Cassidy's in Bolivia, now, Archie, and if this guy was anybody he'd be down there with him, so maybe they were just in a bar together sometime or Cassidy sold him a horse.
LILY. Butch sold *you* a horse, oh that's funny.
HENRY. *(Very cagey.)* Yeah, Cassidy didn't know much about horses, did he, ma'am. The real expert was that doctor's son in the gang. What did your old man do, mister?

ARCHIE. They're *going* to Bolivia, Henry. That's what he came to ask her.

HENRY. Only she won't go. Or I know, she won't go on a horse and he won't go in a car! Is that the holdup, pops?

ARCHIE. Don't give him any ideas, Henry. *(The Outlaw laughs.)*

OUTLAW. Would you like to see a holdup, Archie?

LILY. Come on. Eat your eggs and let's get out of here.

HENRY. Relax, Archie. A holdup is quick. A holdup would be over by now. Unless of course, you forgot how to pull one.

ARCHIE. *(Trying to stay in Henry's good graces.)* Yeah, you're supposed to bust in here. No, first you ride up on your horse. You don't shoot your horse first. *(Expecting Henry to be pleased.)* You ride up on your horse, you slam open the doors, you say everybody does what I say and nobody gets hurt. *(The Outlaw laughs.)* And then you say up against the wall.

HENRY. No wall, Archie.

ARCHIE. The cookshack and spread your arms.

OUTLAW. Situation like this, I'd say down on the ground, Archie.

ARCHIE. Then it's throw your money over here.

OUTLAW. *(Pointing the gun at them.)* All right. Down on the ground, boys. *(They hesitate.)* Now!

LILY. What are you doing?

ARCHIE. Her too?

OUTLAW. I rode a thousand miles to see her. I don't want her dirty.

LILY. If this is for my benefit, you can stop right now because I've seen it, outlaw. Get up, you two. We're leaving right this minute. *(And as she starts to move, the Outlaw grabs her, rough, and pushes her back down on the bench. Archie sees this and ducks his head even further into the ground.)*

ARCHIE. Throw our money over to you?

HENRY. Why don't you just shut up, Archie.

OUTLAW. Yeah, let's have your money.

HENRY. Don't have mine on me.

ARCHIE. Mine's in my bedroll, inside.
OUTLAW. See, Archie? I knew that already.
ARCHIE. She could get it for you.
OUTLAW. I don't need your money.
HENRY. So what are we doin' with our face in the dirt?
OUTLAW. *(Laughs.)* Ask Archie. It was his idea. *(Henry sits up, furious with Archie, slaps him hard with his hat.)*
ARCHIE. Can we sit up?
OUTLAW. Sure.
ARCHIE. *(Aware of Henry's rage.)* Could you just tell us what you want so we could give it to you so you could go on, wherever you're goin?
OUTLAW. Who says I'm goin' anywhere? I'm gettin what I want. A visit. Hear some stories, see some people. I haven't seen any people for a long time.
ARCHIE. Why not?
LILY. Because he acts like this, Archie.
ARCHIE. I mean, what is this? Who are you?
HENRY. You mind your own business.
ARCHIE. This feels like my business to me.
HENRY. It's his past, it's his business.
ARCHIE. I can ask the man.
HENRY. You can shut up!
ARCHIE. Why should I? So he won't know we're scared?
HENRY. I'm not scared. I'm sick to death of you.
ARCHIE. Me? What about him? He's the one ordered you around all night. He's got his gun in our face and you're sick to death of me? I don't get you, Henry.
HENRY. You never have. You don't know a thing about me.
ARCHIE. Oh I get it. If she won't go with him, you will, is that it? You'll just disappear to Bolivia like one of your books come to life and I'll have to tell Mr. White what happened in the morning? Let Dad sit around the rest of his life wondering what ever happened to Henry while I'm out doing your work on the ranch? Well, why don't you tell him how many shots it took you to nail that coyote in the barn last year.

HENRY. *(Slaps him hard.)* And why don't you just remember we're all alone out here. And I've had you hanging around my neck as long as I can remember and if I decide to cut you loose, Diddly, nobody's ever gonna know.

ARCHIE. What does that mean?

OUTLAW. It means he's not on your side, Archie. Nobody is really, when you get right down to it, out here.

LILY. *(Trying a different approach.)* Look, I'm sorry you two got in the middle of this. It's just two old friends getting together someplace safe, all right? We'll be on our way now.

HENRY. He can't go into town, girl. His draw's so shaky he wouldn't last two minutes.

OUTLAW. *(Drawing his gun as he turns.)* Shoot him first?

HENRY. *(Grabbing Archie like a shield.)* Him first!

OUTLAW. That's fine. Get you both with one shot.

HENRY. *(Jumping away from Archie.)* God that was fast! You've still got it all, don't you! Now. Let's see if the kid can dance!

LILY. Now you look here!

OUTLAW. *(Laughs.)* Shoot at his feet, you mean?

ARCHIE. Henry! You're not reading this in some book. What the hell are you doing?

HENRY. Something I should've done a long time ago. Looking out for myself. He needs somebody to ride with him and I'm it! We'll take two of the horses off this place and be on our way.

OUTLAW. *(Quickly throwing Henry a rope.)* You better tie him up so he don't follow us.

HENRY. *(Catches the rope and grabs Archie.)* Yeah boy!

LILY. Tom! Put that gun away! This is ridiculous! *(The Outlaw is just as surprised as she is that Henry is willing to tie Archie up, but he doesn't show Henry that.)*

ARCHIE. What did I ever do to you?

HENRY. Are you kidding? My whole life I spent so you could go to school, so you could dream about airplanes, so you could go to church. I'm out there feedin' half-starved cattle and raisin' scrub crops, still workin' for Dad when I oughta be long gone all because you can't do nuthin' and never could. The most help you can ever be is just get out of my way, Archie. All you ever think about is where your next bath is comin' from and tell 'em, Archie, what are you saving your money for?

LILY. *(Furious.)* I'm leaving right this minute and Archie's coming with me. Get whatever you need and let's get out of here. *(Henry trips Archie to make him fall down and to make it clear that Archie's not going anywhere. He starts to tie him up, and he's real rough about it.)*

ARCHIE. *(An appeal to Lily.)* I'm saving for a buggy. I already ordered the lap robe and harness. *(Then to Henry.)* You watch. You'll want to borrow it. Well don't even ask. I'm gonna be somebody.

HENRY. Somebody's aunt, that's what you'll be. Dad took Archie to the Hart Ranch. They brought in forty-eight hundred head of cattle, Dad picked the hundred he wanted, then they rode with the drivers bringing the cattle back to Clovis. Know what Archie had to say about the trip? The ranch house was dirty.

ARCHIE. Noisy. We slept in a room where a man was killed. There was a bullet hole in the door!

HENRY. *(To the Outlaw.)* See what I mean?

ARCHIE. You coulda gone on that trip except Dad knew you'd get drunk.

HENRY. You ain't goin' nowhere now, kid.

LILY. What kind of man ties up his brother? *(To the Outlaw.)* And you! You ask me to meet you out here in the middle of nowhere after twenty years and then you won't even talk to me. And they don't play this kind of game even in bars anymore. I see this, all right, but it's when the school lets out for recess. Or when we celebrate Frontier Day.

HENRY. There. Done and tight! That's what I felt like my whole life, Archie. How do you like it, huh? *(Kicks him.)*

OUTLAW. *(As Henry is proud of his work, the Outlaw takes his time, coming over to him.)* Now, who are you?

HENRY. What?

OUTLAW. You heard me.

ARCHIE. Why don't you tie yourself up now, Henry.

HENRY. Who am I?
OUTLAW. Hard to say, huh?
HENRY. You mean how old am I?
OUTLAW. Start there, sure.
HENRY. Thirty.
OUTLAW. Go on.
HENRY. Not married. Live at the ranch.
ARCHIE. Lives at home.
OUTLAW. Big ranch?
HENRY. Pretty big.
OUTLAW. You ride?
HENRY. Ride. Good. Good rider, yeah. Rope. Shoot too.
OUTLAW. What.
HENRY. *Shoot* what?
OUTLAW. How's this for "talk," girl? This what you wanted to hear?
HENRY. I shot a Navy Colt before, but a Winchester's what's around most of the time. If you need somebody ... if it's got a safe in it, I know Hercules powder and dynamite.
OUTLAW. Where'd you learn that?
ARCHIE. He didn't. He's lying. He reads Police Gazette in the barber shop.
HENRY. Shut up, Archie, or we'll gag you too.
OUTLAW. Well, you look strong enough all right.
HENRY. Would I be inside or outside? Lookout? Horseholder?
OUTLAW. What are you like, cowboy?
HENRY. What do I like? Same as everybody. Money and a good time.
OUTLAW. No. Something you did once. Where you've been. How you are. How you'd ... be.
HENRY. I don't understand.
ARCHIE. Something you did once, Henry. A story.
HENRY. Deaf Charley and Peep O'Day don't tell stories.
OUTLAW. The're dead.
ARCHIE. More outlaws, I guess.

HENRY. Outlaws, you bet. The Wild Bunch. O'Day was a horseholder. Wasn't he? *(Turning to the Outlaw.)*
ARCHIE. All the outlaws are dead, Henry.
HENRY. *(Vicious.)* What do you know about it, Archie? Shut up!
LILY. Do you want a blanket, Archie? Something to drink?
ARCHIE. *(As Lily comes over to him and moves him out of their way.)* Why don't you go on. This isn't gonna be a very good time, here. I know Henry when he gets like this and there's no stopping him. They won't hurt me. I hate this place.
LILY. Tom, stop this. Come home with me. Wherever you've been, it's been hard, I know, but I want you with me now. We've got some catching up to do.
OUTLAW. *(Interrupting her.)* You gotta tell me *something,* cowboy.
HENRY. You know about Hole-in-the-Wall and I'm gonna tell you about egg hunts as a kid?
OUTLAW. You set traps for em? Trail em through the desert? Use your shotgun, what? I never been on a egg hunt.
ARCHIE. Tell him about breaking horses, tell him about threshing soy beans with a stick. Tell him about your life, Henry.
HENRY. I get thirsty. It's the same thing all the time.
ARCHIE. It has to last longer than that, Henry.
HENRY. Good story would be good company, I guess, at night. Hiding out. *(No response from the Outlaw.)* O.K. I'll tell you about egg hunts and you tell me about Hole-in-the-Wall.
OUTLAW. Go.
HENRY. *(Not enjoying this at all. It looks like school.)* The week before Easter, mother would give us each a dozen eggs, each of us boys, marked so we'd know whose was whose. We'd hide 'em around the farm, this was back in Oklahoma. Then all week we'd look for...
OUTLAW. Hunt.
HENRY. Yeah, hunt. Hunt for each other's eggs and when we found some we'd hide 'em again in a harder place where only we knew so that at the end of the week on Easter morning, the boy

with the most eggs won. Now it's your turn.
OUTLAW. Won what?
HENRY. *(A sudden hostility.)* Just won. If you were smart, you buried your own eggs and ate the other ones you found.
ARCHIE. We knew you were doing that.
OUTLAW. You cheated at egg hunt?
HENRY. I won, didn't I? I wanted to win. *(Now brighter.)* You can start with Flat Nose Currie. Did a horse really kick him in the face?
OUTLAW. Never knew the man. Before my time.
HENRY. Well, when *was* your time?
OUTLAW. I forgot.
HENRY. We made a deal!
OUTLAW. So maybe I'll cheat. You have a Christmas tree?
HENRY. *(Disgusted.)* The man says he's an outlaw and then he asks me about our Christmas tree.
ARCHIE. He's crazy, Henry. It doesn't matter who he is. He doesn't have any gang to take you into. He's just crazy. Tell him about Christmas.
HENRY. You're Tom McCarty, aren't you?
OUTLAW. McCarty is dead. Tell me why you never have any money. Tell me how you done nuthin' for so long, Henry. Tell me why you're still living at home.
HENRY. It's none of your goddamn business!
OUTLAW. Tell me why you tied up your brother. Nobody I know *ever* tied up his brother. Why'd you do that? I mean, we got rules out here for this sort of thing, or used to. Is this how people do now? Cause if it is, I don't want any part of it. I'm goin' right back where I been and I'm stayin' put this time. *(Now as much to Lily as Henry.)* I mean, you drop out of sight for a little while and look what we got for boys now. And you're drivin' a car and talkin' hard, girl.
HENRY. You tell me who you are!
OUTLAW. *(Grinning.)* Kilpatrick.
HENRY. Dead.
OUTLAW. Sundance.

HENRY. Bolivia.
OUTLAW. *(Laughing, mocking.)* Nope. Dead. I'm Billy the Kid. I'm Jesse James. *(Henry pulls his gun, insisting on an answer.)* O.K. cowboy. Now we all saw your gun. Now put it away. *(Henry cocks the pistol.)*
ARCHIE. Please, mister... *(Then to Lily.)* Or you tell. Tell Henry who he is.
OUTLAW. *(Cooling down a little.)* I killed Tom McCarty. That help any?
HENRY. How?
ARCHIE. *(Thinks this is all ridiculous.)* Who is Tom McCarty?
HENRY. Tom McCarty taught Butch Cassidy to rob banks.
LILY. Handsome, funny.
HENRY. They got ten grand outta Telluride.
LILY. The best horse-handler in the business.
HENRY. Tom McCarty was smart!
LILY. Smelled like wild mint and wore a long leather coat, aspen gold.
HENRY. I don't believe you killed him!
LILY. I loved that coat. And a green scarf around his neck. Oh my.
HENRY. Who are you to kill Tom McCarty?
LILY. I figured somebody'd kill him for his money some day, he had so much of it. I should've married him.
ARCHIE. Did he want you to?
OUTLAW. He did.
LILY. Well why didn't he say something. I was crazy for him!
OUTLAW. He was scared.
LILY. You know what you have to do to forget a man like that? You have to buy an automobile, for God's sake.
HENRY. *(Finding the Outlaw's case now.)* How do I know you killed him?
OUTLAW. You don't. But... I got his watch. *(Pitches it to Henry to make him drop the case.)* Maybe I bought it. I got his spurs. Maybe he gave them to me. I got his case, there. Maybe I was his friend.

HENRY. This McCarty's?
LILY. Does it say Forget-me-not, LTK on the back?
HENRY. It does.
LILY. It's McCarty's. I gave it to him.
HENRY. How did you kill him? No. Tell us what happened to his money. She said he had a lot of money. What's in that suitcase?
OUTLAW. Whatever it is, it's mine.
ARCHIE. What a great idea, rob an old guy out in the wheat field.
LILY. There's no money in that case, Henry. It's old wanted pictures, newspaper articles, books about his friends, books with his name in them.
HENRY. He's no outlaw. Some whore sold him that watch. He's just some horse thief, some gone crazy sheepherder. Just a copperhead, prissy-ass grandpa. He sneaked up on the smartest bank robber in the west and shot him in cold blood. A worm, unless I hear different.
ARCHIE. Shut up, Henry.
HENRY. You're gonna tell us how you killed Tom McCarty, *if* you killed Tom McCarty, and then we're gonna tie you up and turn you in. Get a hundred dollars! Outlaw Killer Killed.
OUTLAW. Look cowboy, relax. I apologize for playin' with you like this. I've just turned mean or something. Let's untie the kid here and...
HENRY. *(A serious threat.)* You touch him and you're dead, mister.
OUTLAW. *(Much more carefully.)* That is money in that case. You're absolutely right. I liked your eggs. I'll give you some.
HENRY. *(Fairly contemptuous.)* I'm gonna take it *all*, after you tell me your "story."
OUTLAW. It's not much of a story. McCarty didn't want to hide, and didn't want to run. He asked me to do it.
HENRY. Shoot him?
OUTLAW. Bury him.
ARCHIE. After you shot him.

OUTLAW. I buried him alive. Just outside of Delta, Colorado.

HENRY. *(Quietly, but firmly.)* I know who you are.

OUTLAW. *(Bitterly.)* It's pretty exciting, isn't it?

HENRY. *(His excitement building.)* Well, I think so. They're looking for you all over this country! Nobody knows what happened to you or where you are and you're sitting right here. What do you know about that! I'm taking you in!

OUTLAW. Come and get me then.

HENRY. You don't think I can.

OUTLAW. Listen, Henry, I've done this over and over for twenty years now. I know how it goes. Somebody wants to kill me so they pull a gun. They yell and scream or they sneak up from the back, it doesn't much matter. It never works. *I* live. They, you, end up dead. I swear it's the truth. It's only fair to tell you. Now, you tell me you heard what I said.

HENRY. Well I know what happened at Delta, Colorado. You were holding the horses behind the bank. You heard one shot and you ran. And you've been hiding ever since! Boy are the boys in town gonna be happy to see you at the end of a rope! Swing in the breeze, mister outlaw!

OUTLAW. I don't think I'd take too well to jail, Henry. Just shoot me. I'll get close enough so you don't miss and I'll put my gun in my hand so it looks fair and all.

HENRY. You never even went back to see they got buried, did you?

LILY. Stop this right now! Both of you!

OUTLAW. *(Very firm.)* You know what to do here, Lily. Get out of the way and stand still!

HENRY. Bill and Fred, remember, Archie? Your brother Bill. His boy, Fred. You left their horses for 'em and you ran.

OUTLAW. They'd have done the same thing if it was me in there! That's just how it worked!

HENRY. They shot a man in the bank so they broke through the back door, but you weren't there. So they got on their horses and Freddie boy lit out toward Third Street on that big roan.

OUTLAW. Gelding. Suzy.

HENRY. You *don't* know what happened, do you? Well, how could you if you've been hiding ever since. This is some story, Archie. Some guy Simpson shot Freddie boy right through his left ear, loaded his gun, got where he had a better aim at Bill and took the back of his head clean off. Scalped him!

OUTLAW. You shut up! You read about me while you got your hair cut.

HENRY. The shot blew Bill right out of the saddle, but Fred's body kept riding around til somebody plugged the horse in the belly. Damn strong horse though. Made it all the way to the post office hitching post where it finally fell down in a big mess of blood, squashed Fred's body underneath, flat as flat. And where were you?

OUTLAW. Shut up! You just shut up!

HENRY. You were riding as fast as you could. Took West Gulch to that little island in the Gunnison River, picked up your fresh horse and disappeared. Left two mighty good fresh horses behind. Did I leave anything out?

OUTLAW. You ... off hoping me or somebody like me would come save you from being a nobody all your life just by sticking a gun in your face.

HENRY. You're a coward! The smartest one of the bunch is nuthin' but a miserable coward!

ARCHIE. Stop it, Henry!

HENRY. I just told him a little story. See, Archie, you don't know all the stories. *(Making a lunge at the Outlaw.)* Now, you're coming with me and...

OUTLAW. Don't touch me, cowboy! *(Henry draws his gun and cocks it, aiming squarely at the Outlaw's back.)*

HENRY. Coward! Coward!

OUTLAW. *(Turns around.)* Why does if have to be you? Why couldn't it be somebody I...

HENRY. What are you waiting for, coward?

OUTLAW. You're asking me to kill you, boy.

HENRY. I'm daring you. You think you can say you're an outlaw and that makes you an outlaw? You ran. Real outlaws, real outlaws...

OUTLAW. It went wrong for me once in my life, Henry. It ain't gone right once for you. All you got in your life is my story to tell.

HENRY. And everybody's gonna know it was me that found you.

OUTLAW. Yeah, that's right. You got one shot. Turn me in and get your name in the paper.

HENRY. And my *picture* with you propped up dead on the ground beside me. Change my whole life.

LILY. He's warned you, Henry. This isn't a game to him! He'll kill you!

HENRY. Yes sir. I've been waitin' for this my whole life. All my miserable hot life!

ARCHIE. Sit down, Henry! He won't shoot you if you sit down!

HENRY. He don't have to fight back. He can just stand there if he wants, but I'm taking all that money. I'm taking you in!

OUTLAW. My brother dies so you can read about it in the barbershop!

ARCHIE. Run, Henry!

HENRY. *(Taking a step toward the Outlaw.)* Nice and easy, now, pops. Throw your gun over there.

OUTLAW. *(Standing still, his hand on his gun.)* I can't do that, cowboy.

HENRY. Then I'm coming after it. You draw and you're dead, mister.

OUTLAW. That's fair. *(And instantly he pulls his pistol and shoots Henry dead.)*

ARCHIE. *(Over Lily's screams.)* Henry!

OUTLAW. *(Taking a step backward.)* He wasn't married, I hope.

ARCHIE. He was my brother!

OUTLAW. I'm sorry.

ARCHIE. You killed my brother!

OUTLAW. He did it himself, really. I'm sorry. You shouldn't draw if you can't shoot.

ARCHIE. *(Straining against the ropes.)* Henry! *(Lily walks over to the Outlaw.)*

LILY. *(In a cold fury.)* Is this what you do now? Ride around daring people to kill you?

OUTLAW. It's not my fault he missed, girl. I stood still, didn't I?

LILY. You are disgusting.

OUTLAW. He didn't give me a chance, honey.

LILY. Give me the gun. Now your knife. Now ... stay put.

OUTLAW. *(As Lily walks over to Archie.)* I'm fine. Just a little ... stiff from riding. *(Lily cuts the ropes tying Archie, Archie gets up quickly and runs to Henry, and, still crying, embraces him, as Lily turns to face the Outlaw.)*

LILY. *(Hands his knife back to him.)* Want to start carving the notch now?

OUTLAW. It was a fair fight.

LILY. He never had a chance and you know it.

OUTLAW. I tried to tell him.

ARCHIE. I tried to tell him.

OUTLAW. Well, then. It was a fair fight.

ARCHIE. *(Standing up, nearly screaming.)* Fair? You told him he would die! That's not *fair*. Fair is when both guys got a chance. Fair is when nobody knows how it will come out! You pulled him right in, didn't you. You dared him! If he could kill you, then he could be somebody.

OUTLAW. Henry wanted to kill an outlaw. Can't kill Indians anymore. Kill an outlaw instead. Everybody out here feels that way. Must be the water.

ARCHIE. What water? *(And he stoops to pick up the gun.)* What's the matter with this country? This isn't what people are supposed to do! He's not supposed to tie me up and you're not supposed to ... He was my brother and he was no good, but now you've gone and killed him! How do you think that makes me feel!

OUTLAW. You have to believe me, Lily. I'm tired of killing these boys, but they won't leave me alone.

ARCHIE. Henry! Henry! *(Lunging across the stage, Archie attacks the Outlaw in a fury of ineffective but desperate punches and kicks which the Outlaw absorbs fairly passively.)*

OUTLAW. I'm sorry, boy. I said I was sorry. Jesus, kid, come on. *(Archie sinks to the ground.)* It's O.K. You're a baby. It's all right. It's all gonna be over in just a little bit.

ARCHIE. Why did you have to come here? Nobody asked you to come here.

OUTLAW. I came to see her.

ARCHIE. *(Not listening to him.)* You didn't have to say anything about being an outlaw.

OUTLAW. I didn't! You did! She did! He did!

ARCHIE. You didn't have to pull that gun and ask for eggs. We'd have given you the eggs. But no! You sit around playing outlaw and my brother ends up dead. You could've lied about the money. If Henry didn't know you had money in that case, he'd have never told that Delta story and he'd still be here! Jesus God. Mother. What am I gonna tell Mother?

OUTLAW. You say this old outlaw wandered into your camp, hungry. He had a sack full of money and Henry wanted it. They fought. Henry died. Simple.

ARCHIE. Simple? Who's gonna believe an old outlaw came here. All the outlaws died.

OUTLAW. I wish.

ARCHIE. Just tell me your name. I have to have something to tell. Just sit down and tell me your name and then you and her can ride off.

OUTLAW. I'm Tom McCarty.

ARCHIE. That's who you said you killed.

OUTLAW. That's right.

ARCHIE. You killed yourself?

OUTLAW. I buried me alive. They killed Bill and Fred and I was the only one left. I gave it up. Disappeared.

LILY. So why didn't you come to me then?

OUTLAW. Because you're exactly where they thought I'd go. I

couldn't put you in that kind of danger and you know it! I had to hide and I did. And then it got harder and harder to show back up, that's all.
ARCHIE. Is there money in that case?
OUTLAW. Forty, fifty thousand. Hard to spend that kind of money out here without attracting attention.
ARCHIE. So give it back.
OUTLAW. I don't know whose it is.
ARCHIE. You know what bank you got it from.
OUTLAW. Banks. Trains. It's a problem.
ARCHIE. What were you doing stealing it if you didn't really want it? What did you think you were going to do with it? You are one sorry outlaw, mister.
OUTLAW. I need a place to sleep, Lily.
LILY. How does prison sound?
ARCHIE. Give me the money. I'll give it to Dad, for Henry.
OUTLAW. It won't help. His son is dead. *(Now trying to be lighter.)* But I gotta admit. "Henry's dead, here's forty-thousand dollars," sounds a helluva lot better than just plain, "Henry"s dead." *(They do not laugh.)* I should've got it in the back. Gunned down on Main Street. But no. I was so smart. I got away.
ARCHIE. I don't want to hear it.
LILY. *(To Archie.)* What are you going to do about Henry? His body.
ARCHIE. We'll bury him. There's three barrels. We'll put him in the barrels and bury him.
LILY. But your mother. Won't she want a funeral? What about the family? Your father won't want to see you without Henry, I bet.
ARCHIE. Well, he's not out here, is he, so I'm making the decision. You want me to watch him be dead til morning? Then what do I do? Carry him home in a sack? It's three days. He'd smell. I'd have to tie him on the horse. He'd fall off. I'd get off, tie him back up, ride on a little bit, he'd fall off again. Three days? No. We'll bury him. *(To the Outlaw.)* But you're gonna dig this grave, "outlaw."

OUTLAW. *(Fiercely.)* I never dug a grave in my life! *(Sees Lily's commanding look.)* But I don't have to go just yet. I could help, I guess.
ARCHIE. You're not going to *help*. You're going to do it.
OUTLAW. *(Still looking at Lily.)* That's what I said.
LILY. That's what I thought you said.
OUTLAW. *(After a moment.)* Good. Ready. Good idea, kid. That's just what I'll do. Dig it as deep as you want, you just tell me. Yes sir. You got a shovel?
ARCHIE. *(Fairly disgusted now.)* Around back, there.
OUTLAW. *(To Lily.)* You just watch and see, girl. Be the nicest grave you ever say. Real comfortable. Be everything a man could want.
LILY. I'll make us some coffee.
OUTLAW. That's a good idea too. Everybody's just full of good ideas. *(And then as they are standing there.)*
ARCHIE. I hate this place. Nobody acts right out here. *(And then aware that they are staring at him.)* Shut up, Archie.
OUTLAW. That's the spirit. *(Wanting to get on with it.)* O.K. One grave, comin' up. *(And the Outlaw heads around the side of the cookshack and Lily starts up the steps into the cookshack and we have.)*

LIGHTS DOWN FOR THE END OF ACT I

ACT II

Lights come up as the Outlaw is shoveling the last dirt in on Henry buried in the barrels. A mound of dirt has formed, Center Stage. Archie sits back, quite disturbed but not saying anything. The Outlaw seems invigorated by his physical labor.

OUTLAW. *(Resting on the shovel.)* There. All done. Rest in Peace. *(To Archie.)* Want a cross or anything? Marker? *(No response.)* I could make one outta...

LILY. Tell him what you want, Archie. Do you want a marker?

ARCHIE. No. Just be in the way. The boys, coming back in the morning, still drunk, they'd trip over it. *(His anger building.)* It's in the wrong place anyway. You dug the grave in the wrong place. This is right where we sit down to eat.

OUTLAW. Why didn't you say that before?

ARCHIE. I didn't want you to stop digging.

OUTLAW. I'll do another one if you want. Just getting used to the shovel, really. How about over there?

ARCHIE. I want a funeral.

LILY. You need a family and a preacher for a funeral. If you'd wanted a funeral, you should've taken him home.

OUTLAW. *(Still so cooperative.)* I'll dig him back up.

ARCHIE. *(To Lily.)* We're having a funeral. I'm the family. He's the preacher.

OUTLAW. I killed him. I can't preach over him too. Wouldn't be right.

ARCHIE. If we were doing what was right around here, you'd be locked up by now. You dug the grave and now you're gonna preach the funeral. And then you're gonna get the hell out of here and you're gonna take her with you.

OUTLAW. No sir.

LILY. You're preaching the funeral all right, but I'm not going with you when you're through.

OUTLAW. Yes you are too, girl. That's what I came for.

LILY. Why didn't you say that right off? We could be in my bed by now. Asleep, by now. We didn't need to see your Wild West Show.

OUTLAW. What did you think I wanted if I didn't want you?

LILY. I have my own life now, Tom. And if I had any thoughts about going with you, which I might have had, seeing you early on tonight, I've sure forgot 'em all now, after what you did. Now, you owe this boy a funeral and I'm staying just long enough to see that he gets it and then I'm getting in my car and going back to town and tell the sheriff you're out here, in case he's interested. You're dangerous. And, I might have been in love with you once, but now... I'm a good citizen.

OUTLAW. Well why did you come out here, then?

LILY. I didn't believe you were still alive.

OUTLAW. *(Furious and hurt.)* And that's the only reason you came all the way out here? You were curious? You just had to know if the old desert rat died or not. Well I sure hope you're satisfied, girl. Contrary to popular opinion and in spite of everything I've tried, I am still alive. *(Quickly to Archie.)* All right. What do I say?

ARCHIE. You're the preacher.

OUTLAW. *(His anger taking another direction.)* We had a good time together, in case you forgot.

LILY. I remember.

OUTLAW. I'm the only man, man enough for you, girl. I'm exactly what you need.

LILY. I need, a whole night's sleep and a hot bath and a month's vacation someplace green and a glass of gin a couple more bartenders and running water, but I don't need you. And I don't know who does. You were mighty entertaining all those years ago, but we've got traveling comedians now and a circus once a year and I guess Pancho Villa could probably use a broken down gunslinger, but other than that I just don't know. You even look better on the wall anymore.

OUTLAW. I took my time getting back here, I'll grant you that. But I've seen these new people. There's nothing to 'em. All talk. *(Looking directly at Archie.)*

ARCHIE. *(Has heard enough.)* We're having a goddamn funeral. Now will you get on with it! Preach!

LILY. Watch your language, Archie.

OUTLAW. I wish it was me there instead of him.

ARCHIE. That ain't what I had in mind.

OUTLAW. It's the truth.

ARCHIE. You start out, "Family and friends..."

OUTLAW. *(Stalling.)* If he'd killed me, would you make him preach over me?

ARCHIE. Henry? He'd have drug your body into town to have it's picture took by now.

OUTLAW. Well, if you're gonna take a picture, it's good to do it quick.

ARCHIE. Will you get on with this! I'm managin' to stay calm right now, but I'm not sure how long it's gonna last.

OUTLAW. If you think you might get really mad, I'll wait.

ARCHIE. So you can kill me too? Uh-uh. Preach or go.

OUTLAW. *(Looking at Lily, hoping to see her change her mind as he preaches.)* I'll preach. *(To Lily.)* You sing. *(She starts to hum.)* Friends and family. Here lies Henry ... *(He looks to Archie.)* Middle name?

ARCHIE. Jackson.

OUTLAW. Tucker. Born?

ARCHIE. 1884, Thomas, Oklahoma.

OUTLAW. Moved to...

ARCHIE. Clovis when he was twelve. Lived there ever since.

OUTLAW. He just had a short time on this earth, but he spent it, well, to tell the truth, he pretty much wasted it.

ARCHIE. *(Objecting.)* Hey!

OUTLAW. But it was his time. And if he wanted to waste it, well that was his business. His business was ... *(He looks to Archie.)* ranchin'? *(Archie nods yes.)* And he was real good at the stuff you had to be a real sunuvabitch to do. Lie, cheat, steal.
ARCHIE. Go on. You're doin' just fine.
OUTLAW. He was bored so he read outlaw books. And he hated himself, but he took it out on everybody else. Now he's dead. Leavin' behind a mother and father? *(Archie nods yes.)* Some brothers and some other family, I guess and maybe some children, who knows? They might miss him, but I wouldn't know why. So, rest in peace, Henry Tucker. The rest of us sure will now that you're gone, so you might as well. You didn't have much love for this brother of yours, Archie, but he done more for you than you would have for him had I killed him instead of you and I want you to take note of that. *(Bitter, personal.)* You didn't have to die, I tried to tell you that, but you didn't listen. Well, you were gonna die anyway, we all are, someday. But you were lucky. You had help. Unlike me. Yes sir, Henry Tucker, things are pretty bad when you can't count on somebody else to kill you. Dyin' just ain't something you should have to do for yourself.
ARCHIE. You're gettin' off the track here.
OUTLAW. O.K. Heaven and hell. I've got some bad news for you, Henry. But you might as well hear it right now, cause you're gonna be findin' it out for yourself pretty soon. I've been thinking about Heaven and Hell a lot here lately, like how they decide where to put you, and I think what it is, is that they put you in a big room forever with people exactly like you, how you were in life, I mean. And that's what makes it heaven or hell. Now you, you hated yourself, like I said, so it's gonna be hell. You'll be in with a whole bunch of ranch hands that never amounted to nuthin' and died mad.
ARCHIE. I got something to say. I didn't ... we didn't get along, you and me, Henry, but you're my brother and I respect that. Rest in peace. *(Goes on, knowing they expect more from him.)* Lotta times I thought I was ready to kill you, Henry, and I know you really did try to drown me at least twice, so no, I didn't care much for you, but I sure didn't like seein' you die. Tell you what, Henry, the story I'm

gonna tell about how you died, it's gonna be some story when I get through with it. If you're ever listening, you're gonna be real proud. I think that's about all I can do for you now. *(To the Outlaw.)* Now, finish up.

OUTLAW. *(Wants this to be over.)* That's it. I didn't know him.

ARCHIE. We need something from the Bible.

LILY. "Man that is born of woman is of few days and full of trouble."

OUTLAW. God that's gloomy. Where'd you pick that up?

LILY. At my rancher's funeral. You've never read the Bible in your life. What do you know?

ARCHIE. "The Lord is my shepherd, I shall not want."

OUTLAW. Are we through now? I ain't prayin to no sheepherder.

ARCHIE. "For yea, though I walk through the valley of the shadow of death I will fear no evil, for thou art with me. Thou preparest a table before me in the presence of mine enemies, my cup runneth over."

ARCHIE and LILY. "Surely goodness and mercy shall follow me all the days of my life and I shall dwell in the house of the Lord forever."

OUTLAW. Dust to dust, an eye for a tooth.

LILY. *(Not pleased with the Outlaw's offering.)* Say you feel bad. Say you're sorry.

OUTLAW. I *am* sorry. I don't know anything to say. I'm lonelier than I thought.

ARCHIE. Pray.

OUTLAW. I don't know how.

ARCHIE. Well, what do you want said at your funeral? Say that.

OUTLAW. What do I want said at my funeral? How bout, "O.K. boys, Reload!"

LILY. I don't believe this! You're not a bit sorry about this. This is just one more dumb boy that missed. What did I ever see in you? This is not a joke, here. This is a dead boy in the ground. Oh I wasted so much time waiting for you. Well no more! This is the end. I am free of you for good and Praise the Lord for it.

OUTLAW. I am sorry. *(Louder.)* I'm sorry, Henry. *(Genuine.)* I really am sorry. I never stayed this long at a killing. *(Getting crazed.)* I'm sorry. *(Reaching quickly into his pocket.)* O.K. I'll show you, Henry Tucker. *(Swallowing the stuff he took from his pcoket.)* That's how sorry I am.

LILY. What was that?

OUTLAW. I sure am sorry. I'm also jealous. You got something I want, Henry, so I'm comin' after you. Archie figured out what to do with you and I trust him to figure out what to do with me. It's not in your honor, Henry, it's just that now that you're gone, it feels like family and a man should die at home. *(To Lily and Archie.)* There! How's that for sorry! That was morphine. I've killed myself!

ARCHIE. *(Contemptuous.)* Well, that really is sorry.

LILY. Anything for a little excitement, huh Tom?

ARCHIE. Yeah, how do we know it was morphine?

OUTLAW. You don't. Why don't you just wait and see. Sit down. Who is the sheriff now anyway?

LILY. Nobody you'd know. Kid from St. Louis. Don't worry about him. He thinks you're dead.

OUTLAW. I wasn't worried. What ever happened to Daisy?

LILY. *(Lunging at him.)* Throw it up! You're going to throw it up! *(He fights her as she's trying to get her finger down his throat.)* Go ahead, bite me! Vomit! You can't do this!

ARCHIE. So this is an outlaw. This is how outlaws die.

OUTLAW. *(Breaking away from Lily.)* Nobody knows how to die, boy.

LILY. How much did you take?

OUTLAW. *(Pacing, raging.)* Nobody knows how to shoot any more either! You'd think just one of these lousy cowboys could... *(Then like a drunken comrade.)* See, Archie, the problem with hiding, is there's nothing to do. *(Then back to Lily.)* God I loved you, woman.

LILY. It's a little late for that, Tom.

OUTLAW. After I go here, Archie, shoot me, just once, don't

overdo it, and turn me in. There's gotta still be a reward out somewhere. Buy yourself ... something ... Buick, something. *(Getting groggy now.)*

LILY. *(Pacing.)* How many times did I get asked to get married? Only once. And you heard about that and came chasing across the country to shoot him. Then did you ask me to marry you? Or come with you even? No! You take off and I don't see you for another ten years. That rancher was rich!

OUTLAW. You got rich on your own, girl.

LILY. *(Angry.)* Yes I did.

OUTLAW. See? Say thank you.

ARCHIE. I'd leave the two of you alone, but I can't see sitting out in the wheat all night. I've got no place to go.

OUTLAW. I know how you feel. Same here.

LILY. *(Beginning to believe it.)* Did you take enough to kill you? Goddamn you. You never even asked me to go to Bolivia with you. You just talked about it and then killed yourself!

ARCHIE. *(As the Outlaw slumps a little.)* Why didn't you take the morphine out in the desert? Big bravery this is. Take it where there's people to see you, cry over you. You make me sick!

OUTLAW. *(Trying to defend himself.)* I went back to Hole-in-the-Wall and I didn't know anybody and there were ... fences, everywhere and I couldn't do it. And I'm dying in front of Lily because I want her to have my money. Not like she needs it, of course, but well ... *(A silly, drugged smile on his face.)* she's who I thought of first. It's time for it, that's all.

ARCHIE. I should've helped Henry shoot you. What kind of thing is this to do to her?

OUTLAW. *(Enjoying the physical sensation the drug has produced.)* If you'll just shut up, this will all be over. How am I supposed to sleep with you yelling at me?

ARCHIE. *(Irritated at the Outlaw's pleasure.)* Putting on quite a show, aren't you? Well, I don't feel a bit sorry for you. Go ahead. Go to sleep. Things getting dark yet?

OUTLAW. Hey, this is pretty nice, here. Just about perfect way to die, seems to me. It don't hurt ... there's no mess to clean up. My heart's on this side, here. Put it right here.

ARCHIE. *(Furious at the vanity.)* Keep your head clean for the picture?

OUTLAW. *(To Lily, much more quiet.)* The doctor gave it to me when I broke my leg last year. He said, *(An uncomfortable laugh.)* "You take this all at once, McCarty, it'll kill you, so go easy." I didn't take any of it. I thought I might get... the horse might fall on me sometime out where ... *(Beginning to have trouble talking now.)* where I couldn't get to ... nobody around to help me and might not want to ... couldn't just wait for it ... or if you didn't want me ... weren't around ... *(The Outlaw drifts off here for a moment, his speech getting very slurred at the end of this speech. There is a sudden, awesome quiet and they both know he has really taken the morphine - something about the way his body looks leaning against the cookshack. Lily backs away and Archie seems hypnotized by the sight of him. Lily finally turns to Archie, there is no pleading, there is simply a decision to be made. Archie looks at her, then back at the Outlaw and then to Henry's grave.)*

ARCHIE. Salt water will do it. If we can get it down him. *(Starting for the Outlaw.)* Well go on! It's inside somewhere. *(Lily rushes for the cookshack. Archie grabs the Outlaw and jerks him up.)* Get up you! Sit up!

OUTLAW. *(Jolted awake.)* You don't have to squeeze. I'm not going anywhere.

ARCHIE. What am I doing?

OUTLAW. I was about to ask you that.

ARCHIE. *(Yelling to Lily.)* He killed my brother. I can't save his life!

LILY. *(Yelling back.)* Where's the water?

ARCHIE. Oh, hell, it's out here.

LILY. *(Rushing out.)* Where?

ARCHIE. On the ground. All we had was in the barrels. Take too long to draw another bucket. Get some vinegar.

LILY. And salt? It'll kill him!

OUTLAW. Bring it on.

ARCHIE. Get it. *(Lily goes back inside.)*

OUTLAW. Dark. Things are dark.
ARCHIE. It's night. Things are dark at night.
OUTLAW. My feet feel real heavy.
ARCHIE. Your boots are heavy. Your feet are in your boots. Your feet only feel heavy.
OUTLAW. That's what I said.
ARCHIE. *(Yelling in to Lily.)* What are you doing in there? Come on!
LILY. *(Coming out with the salt and a big unmarked can.)* It's dark in there. This is something sloshy, but I don't know what. Could be cherries or beans ... Got an opener?
OUTLAW. If I wanted my life saved. I picked the wrong crew.
ARCHIE. On the wall over the stove.
LILY. I looked already. You go.
ARCHIE. *(Handing the Outlaw over to her.)* Jesus God! *(Rushing for the cookshack.)*
LILY. You cold?
OUTLAW. Yeah. You know what happened to my coat?
LILY. I loved that coat.
OUTLAW. Dirty little Navaho took it. Stole it. Stole my coat. Little boy...
LILY. *(To Archie.)* Hurry up in there!
ARCHIE. *(Running out, having opened the can.)* Coming. Hold his head back. Come on, Tom. Open up, now, drink this.
LILY. What is it? *(As the Outlaw swallows some, chokes immediately and throws it up.)* Ah ... tomatoes.
ARCHIE. Once more, Tom. You did just fine. *(He forces more down his throat with the same result.)* I just had a bath, too.
OUTLAW. Taste ... mouth ... Get ... *(As he tries to reach in his pocket.)*
ARCHIE. I'll get it. What am I looking for?
OUTLAW. Mint.
ARCHIE. *(Looking at Lily.)* Women really like this mint smell, huh? *(Finding some, putting it in the Outlaw's mouth.)*
OUTLAW. I like it. *(Then he chokes again.)*

ARCHIE. We have to walk around. Keep him moving. We can't let him sit anymore. *(Shoulders the Outlaw.)* You're gonna talk, you. You're gonna tell me your whole life story. Now, where were you born? Got any children? What color hair did your mother have?
OUTLAW. I'm all right. Just ... late ... tired...
ARCHIE. *(Slaps him.)* You're dying. You're dead if you don't keep moving. Kick your leg. Here! *(Kicks it for him.)* Kick. Kick. *(Archie's feet get tangled in the Outlaw's feet and they both fall.)* Oh God. *(Trying to get a rise out of him.)* They'll write about this. You killing yourself. How's that going to sound? Last Outlaw Kills Self.
OUTLAW. Bad. Sound bad ... Lily...
LILY. Look at me, Tom.
OUTLAW. Pretty.
LILY. We can save you if you'll help us. You threw some up but there's still plenty left in you. You have to keep moving. Stay awake.
ARCHIE. Do you want us to save you? We have to know right now.
OUTLAW. I don't want to die. Don't let me die...
ARCHIE. *(Again trying to force him to talk.)* Why not? Why shouldn't we let you die? You killed my brother and who knows who else? You've obviously been thinking about it. Yes or no? Die or not.
OUTLAW. Not. Not. Archie. Please. Lily...
ARCHIE. *(Pulling Lily away from him.)* Prove it. Stand up. Stand up and we'll save you. Why do you want to live? You didn't a few minutes ago, and things haven't changed all that much.
OUTLAW. *(Trying to talk.)* Pretty.
ARCHIE. Pretty! That's why you want to live? Because she's pretty?
OUTLAW. *(Making it, standing up.)* Up, Live. *(And immediately, he falls back into Archie's arms.)*
ARCHIE. She's a whole lot better than pretty. Walk. Walk.
LILY. Give me his other arm. *(As they shoulder the Outlaw between them.)*

ARCHIE. *(After a moment.)* You cold?

LILY. Freezing.

ARCHIE. I don't know what I can do. I'd get you a coat but ... he'd fall. *(She nods.)* I know. Take his coat.

LILY. Good. Cold might pick him up some. *(They struggle to take his jacket off as they continue to talk.)*

ARCHIE. That'd be good. We save him and you die of pneumonia.

LILY. You're cold too.

ARCHIE. Yep. Sure am. And so is Henry. That makes four of us. All cold. *(And Archie has awkward boyish awareness that now the two of them have to talk for what might be hours.)*

LILY. Archie ... I'm sorry about Henry.

ARCHIE. *(Not wanting to talk about it, starts to walk the Outlaw around again.)* Henry used to make Mother so mad. We'd be in church and Henry and some of his buddies would sneak up to the wagons parked out front. There'd be babies or little kids sleeping in the wagons and they'd switch the babies. People got home and found they had the right blanket with the wrong baby in it.

LILY. Is that how you got in your family in the first place?

ARCHIE. *(Surprised that she guessed this.)* That's what Henry says. Dad too when he's mad at me. Which is always. I don't mind, really. You gotta have a mean streak like you gotta have a mule out here.

LILY. You don't have that mean streak, Archie.

ARCHIE. *(Doesn't want to talk about that either.)* Dad wanted an orchard like we had back in Oklahoma. But the ground was so hard, we had to put dynamite in each hole to shake the dirt loose so the roots could take hold. Dad made me haul water on a sled for two years to keep those peach trees alive.

LILY. Did they make it?

ARCHIE. No. He's mostly raising cattle now. He's got this fool idea that the government's gonna need mules for the war, so he's just bought fifteen wild mares to start breedin' em.

LILY. There could be money in that.

ARCHIE. Hell, the war's gonna be over before the mules are old enough to sell.

LILY. You're old enough to leave home, Archie, find a place that suits you better. What are you waiting for?

ARCHIE. I can't leave, Lily, I was born here. Did Tom really shoot your husband?

LILY. We're all at the church. Saloon's even closed for the event. Roy Luther, tending bar, said he wouldn't believe I'd get married unless he saw it himself. Tom came in late. Sat at the back. Nobody saw him.

ARCHIE. But when the preacher said, "Anybody got any reason why I shouldn't marry these two," Tom stepped out in the aisle, said "Draw Mister," and shot him.

LILY. Actually no, the rancher shot first, but Tom is quick, you know.

ARCHIE. I know.

LILY. He came by later. Said he rode three straight days to get there. Said they'd be after him so he had to go.

ARCHIE. Got on his horse and rode off.

LILY. Well, not right away, no. And the town, they didn't send a posse, after all. People knew the rancher was about to buy a herd of sheep and it got to be a joke. Roy Luther said I really did know how to take care of a sheepherder, all right. The town painted my house for me, to say thanks. *(A pause.)* I thought Tom was dead. The man just disappears.

ARCHIE. But he wants people to know him.

LILY. Well, he doesn't want to be forgotten, that's true. But he doesn't want to be recognized and shot either.

ARCHIE. What he wants is you.

LILY. *(Interrupting, fast.)* He wants it to be like it was. Every sheriff in...

OUTLAW. *(Stirs at the word sheriff, stands on his own, ready to fight, then breaks away from them, charging around.)* Sheriff! God, it's Hazen! I can smell him he's so close! *(Crouching as if in battle.)* Reload!

LILY. *(Sensing immediately what to do.)* There's no way out! There must be twenty!

OUTLAW. *(Now creeping around as if behind rocks.)* Keep firing ... one at a time ... slip through. Take Teapot north. *(Now slumping as quickly as he awaked before.)* Brakeman ... shoulda killed the brakeman.
LILY. *(Slapping him.)* Tom! Tom! *(But he doesn't recover.)* That's how we have to do it! Who else is there? *(Then quickly, yelling at the Outlaw.)* Jim Averill! It's Cattle Kate! We got a mess comin', honey!
OUTLAW. *(Charging around again, firing his gun.)* The Regulators! Is it the Regulators?
ARCHIE. *(Wanting to help.)* It's the Regulators!
OUTLAW. You're not taking me, Robert Connor. I got you Bothwell! *(Grabs Archie as if to strangle him, then collapses and they both fall. Archie pulls the Outlaw up to sit on the ground, Archie on the bench behind him. He massages his face and neck, trying to think of some way to continue the conversation with Lily, as she is momentarily out of breath.)*
ARCHIE. So. Were you really a whore or not?
LILY. *(Quite annoyed.)* What difference does it make? You wouldn't be helping me if I were?
ARCHIE. No, I just meant, well, you don't seem like, you know...
LILY. No, I don't know.
ARCHIE. If you were a whore, then...
LILY. You might be wrong about whores, huh? You might be in big trouble if you had the money?
ARCHIE. *(Eager to change the subject.)* Tom! Hey Tom! *(Then to Lily.)* Come on. All I know is Remember the Alamo.
LILY. Frank Canton!
OUTLAW. *(Jerking up instantly.)* Kill Frank Canton! Come out here, Frank Canton!
ARCHIE. *(Yelling.)* They got him, McCarty!
OUTLAW. Got who?
ARCHIE. I can't tell!
OUTLAW. *(Losing consciousness.)* Nate? They got Nate?
ARCHIE. *(Attempting to revive him.)* It was Nate all right!

OUTLAW. *(Reviving.)* Light those fires, Brown. Burn 'em to Kingdom Come! *(Then falling, unconscious. Archie knows, by now, not to let him charge off by himself in these moments of being awake. As a result, Archie is dragged around the stage, as the Outlaw relives his past. They put him between them and begin to walk again.)*
ARCHIE. *(Trying again, this time more carefully.)* Were you born out here?
LILY. I don't talk about my life. It sounds like one of those books.
ARCHIE. I got it. Your family came out here homesteading and they got wiped out in a drought and your mother died having a baby so your daddy left to join up with the Mexican army, leaving you in the house alone. Some preacher's wife took you in and raised you til they died in a fire at a barn raisin'. They left you everything they had, which was two oil lamps and a Bible, so you moved to the city and got ... work.
LILY. *(Has to laugh.)* Very good. You've been reading the books. *(Archie is pleased.)* Your mother is ... uh ... a little fat lady who wears her hair in braids wrapped around her head and sits out on the stoop at night to wash her feet before she goes to bed.
ARCHIE. That's her all right. When I think about her, away from home like this, all I see is a big white apron. She pays me ten cents for every turkey nest I find. Turkeys hide their nests, you know.
LILY. *(Distracted.)* No. I didn't know. *(Yelling again.)* Hainer's gonna give himself up!
OUTLAW. *(Charging out of his unconsciousness.)* Claverly, you lay one hand on me ... I'll kill you. I'll give you all six of these and then I'll bash your ... *(Then collapsing again.)*
LILY. *(Defeated, worried.)* Why did he do this? How are we supposed to go on? I can't do this all night. I don't know any more names. Why, Tom?
ARCHIE. But where did you get the money for the hotel?
LILY. *(Suddenly depressed and bitter.)* It's none of your damn business.
ARCHIE. I know what you did! It was a big ranch. You sold it!

LILY. And everything on it! Kicked out the whores and turned the place into a hotel. That rancher was rich. I had money left. I built a school. I named it for the rancher. Least I could do, you know. *(Irritated again.)* Don't you even know one sheriff's name? One deputy?

ARCHIE. *(Stares at the Outlaw, then yells.)* Daniel Boone! *(The Outlaw slumps even more.)* Sorry.

LILY. No. I'm sorry. Nobody knows those names anymore. Just as well, I guess. It wasn't as much fun as we said it was.

ARCHIE. I bet you didn't get too many proposals after what Tom did.

LILY. *(Very hostile.)* Can't we talk about something else?

ARCHIE. Look. I know you're scared. But he'll make it. You'll see. His pulse is stronger already. Don't you think?

LILY. I don't know how to take it.

ARCHIE. You just count. You remember if you're counting faster than you did when you counted before.

LILY. I didn't count before.

ARCHIE. *(Much too cheerful for Lily.)* So you'll count next time. I counted before. I think he just might make it.

LILY. And then what?

ARCHIE. And then what?

LILY. No, you don't say what I said. You say something new.

ARCHIE. I don't know what to say. I don't know what we're talking about.

LILY. So what *do* you know? Ever had a beer, Archie?

ARCHIE. No.

LILY. Ever seen a girl without any clothes on?

ARCHIE. Just my little sister.

LILY. It's not the same, you know.

ARCHIE. Yeah. It's different.

LILY. Real different. So what *have* you been doing?

ARCHIE. Don't make fun of me. You won't tell me anything, so I won't tell you anything either. And I know a lot of good stories. I could fill up this whole night telling you my life. How I learned to rope calves or the time Bill got his hand eat by a catfish. *(Gets tickled in spite of himself at this memory.)* But I'm not telling! It's private! What do you care anyway?

LILY. I have everything all set and then he just drops in and tries to kill himself. And we're trying to save him! And all you know is stories. Well, you'll get a good one out of this, won't you?

ARCHIE. Do you want him to live or not, because if you don't, then I'm a damn fool carrying him around all night. He killed my brother!

LILY. *That's* what we're talking about. He's a killer.

ARCHIE. I'll drop him on the ground right now if you say to.

LILY. You would not either.

ARCHIE. Go sit then. See what happens.

LILY. We should turn him in.

ARCHIE. Let's save his life first.

LILY. No. Now. While he's asleep. Let's put him in my car and take him into town an turn him in.

ARCHIE. He'd die on the trip. If you want him to live, we have to keep walking.

LILY. That car is the only reason we even stayed here two minutes, isn't it? He wouldn't ride in my car! Outlaws don't ride in cars, I guess. Well how's he going to get around anymore? What is he going to do if we save him?

ARCHIE. What will you do if we don't?

LILY. I'll do just fine! You give me one good reason for saving his life! It's over anyway and he knows it. That's why he pulled this stunt.

ARCHIE. You were his last chance, Lily. He had to take it.

LILY. Yours is the life worth saving here. If you leave right now, you can hop that early train. When the crew comes back tomorrow, I'll explain everything and you'll be on your own.

ARCHIE. I couldn't just disappear, Lily.

LILY. There's nothing for you here except winding up like Henry.

ARCHIE. I'm nothing like Henry and you know it.

LILY. Not now you aren't, but you wait. You'll get his work now that he's gone, won't you? It was that work that killed him. You'll

dry up, Archie, just like he did.
ARCHIE. I'll get his share of the ranch, too, if I do his work.
LILY. Is that what you want, Archie? Twice as much desert to blow away. Your mother can get along without you. What are you so afraid of?
ARCHIE. Was that story true, about Delta, Colorado?
LILY. Yeah. Roy Luther told me the same thing. He ran away. Fast as he could.
ARCHIE. But why?
LILY. To get away, Archie. To live. So he could hide. It's not fair. I hate it.
ARCHIE. There's no way you can *hide* out here. I stand in the middle of our land and I think the only way out is straight up. I can see for fifty miles in any direction. I mean, if I could be in two places at once, I could ride a horse for a whole day and see myself. *(Lily doesn't understand.)* I could see where I started from where I got to after riding all day. The only thing that ever really gets out of where we live is the train.
OUTLAW. *(Sudden, unprovoked.)* Bill! Fred! *(Then falling back into her arms.)*
ARCHIE. Good! He woke up on his own that time!
LILY. *(Almost tenderly.)* Whenever they were planning to rob a bank, Tom would always work a local ranch for a few months first. Get to know the town, you know. I always thought some of those ranchers missed his working their horses more than they missed their money in the bank. I guess he thought I'd bring him some beautiful horse to ride back tonight. I just ... didn't think about it. I ... forgot.
ARCHIE. What was it like when you ... the old days, with him?
LILY. He'd blow in like the breath of God, horse sleek and black, and all you'd see was his flyin' coat and this big hat, and he'd make everybody else I'd ever met look real tired. And he knew you wanted him, and you did. Soon as you saw him you had to have him. That's still true. That's what happened to Henry.
ARCHIE. He'll make it. We'll pull him out of this. And then all

you have to do is take that new picture he's got for you and burn it. Henry was an expert and Henry wouldn't have recognized him if Tom hadn't said Delta, Colorado, Bill and Fred.

LILY. He would never let me do that, Archie. You saw how proud he was of that new picture.

ARCHIE. So burn it.

LILY. But then what do I do with him? Drug his coffee when he gets mean?

ARCHIE. He loves you. He's old and he needs you.

LILY. But what about me? I'm not as old as he is. I'm not through yet!

ARCHIE. I don't blame him for wanting to look at you again.

LILY. He could've just asked me to send him a picture.

ARCHIE. No, I mean it. Your skin looks so soft.

LILY. And I have all the softest parts covered up. You should see *them. (She means this to sound irritated, so she is just as surprised as Archie when it comes out so seductively.)*

ARCHIE. Now why did you say that?

LILY. Sounds good, huh?

ARCHIE. I just never heard it before, that's all.

LILY. You really are a virgin, huh? Saving yourself for some church girl could be a real mistake, Archie.

ARCHIE. Dad says not to worry about it. There's nothing to it.

LILY. Dad ... is wrong.

ARCHIE. *(After a moment.)* Well, if you want to tell me something I should know, you know, just one or two little things just to get me started...

OUTLAW. *(Eyes opening, slowly gaining consciousness.)* Lily?

ARCHIE. He's alive!

LILY. *(Smiling at Archie.)* Right here, Tom.

OUTLAW. Archie?

ARCHIE. *(Really pleased.)* You bet.

OUTLAW. Henry?

ARCHIE. No Henry.

OUTLAW. Oh that's right. I'm sorry.

ARCHIE. We've been through that already.

LILY. Can you sit up?

ARCHIE. *(Reaching in the Outlaw's pocket.)* Got something for you, old man. Nice piece of mint. Gonna cut that bad taste in your mouth. Here, open up. *(Taking some for himself.)* Thanks. Don't mind if I do.

LILY. I never knew how he got that mint smell. I don't think it grows wild around here. He must have it planted somewhere.

ARCHIE. From what I feel in his pocket, he could have it planted in there. *(She laughs.)* Tastes good. I see why he likes it.

OUTLAW. What happened?

LILY. You tried to kill yourself. You took the morphine.

ARCHIE. You threw some of it up. That's tomatoes there on your coat. And we walked the rest of it out of you.

OUTLAW. Why did you do that? It would be all over by now.

ARCHIE. You asked us to. You said don't let me die.

OUTLAW. Well, damn.

ARCHIE. We saved your life. You should say more than well, damn.

OUTLAW. You're some kid, Archie. You walked for me all night, and now you're gonna talk for me all day. What do you want me to say?

ARCHIE. Ask Lily to marry you.

OUTLAW. I can't. I don't have any money.

ARCHIE. You've got a suitcase full of money!

OUTLAW. No.

ARCHIE. There's forty-fifty thousand dollars in that case!

OUTLAW. I said No. Look for yourself. *(Archie goes over and opens the suitcase. He bends over it, looks through several layers and closes the suitcase without saying anything, but we must know he is shocked by what he sees.)* I'm so sleepy.

ARCHIE. *(Very sympathetic.)* We wore you out, I guess. Kicked you, punched you, slapped you. Fought the Pinkertons with you all night. You took a real beating all right. *(To Lily.)* Is it O.K. for him to sleep now?

LILY. I think so. I think it would be good. There's still a few hours left before morning.
ARCHIE. You were going to ask Lily to marry you.
OUTLAW. You saved my life. I owe you something. *(To Lily.)* Lily, I've always loved you. I'm not much anymore. Will you have me? Will you marry me?
LILY. *(A fairly serious look.)* What do you think, Archie? Should I marry this outlaw?
ARCHIE. *(Beaming.)* It was my idea!
LILY. I think you're right. Yes, Tom, I'll marry you. But it better be tomorrow or I don't ever want to see you again.
OUTLAW. I can't live in town.
LILY. I have a farm. There's a house. There are horses.
OUTLAW. Good horses?
LILY. Not yet.
ARCHIE. That's your part. You got work to do when you wake up.
OUTLAW. Farm. *(And he drifts off into what looks like normal sleep.)*
LILY. We should sleep too. I feel terrible.
ARCHIE. I feel great! I never saved anybody's life before. The way I feel, I could thresh this whole field myself before they get back.
LILY. *(Enjoying his thrill.)* I bet you could, Archie.
ARCHIE. We did it! We saved his life! We really did it! The fight was Henry's fault anyway, mostly. He got to telling that story and things just got all out of hand. Tom tried to tell Henry not to come after him. Why, as far as Tom's concerned, it was just about self-defense, don't you think?
LILY. I'm not thinking about it.
ARCHIE. Saving somebody's life! That's got to be the best feeling in the whole world.
LILY. It's in the top three anyway.
ARCHIE. Did you see, Tom even knew my name when he woke up. He'll have you, that farm, those horses. He'll have a whole new life. And you, you'll have him. You sure he's all right here?

LILY. He's out til morning, I'm sure. How old are you, Archie?
ARCHIE. Seventeen.
LILY. *(Standing up.)* That's old enough. I need a favor.
ARCHIE. Well you just name it! I done all I could for both of them and they neither one deserved it probably. So you just tell me what it is and I'll do it.
LILY. I want you to take me in the cookshack or wherever your bed is, someplace warm where...
ARCHIE. God, yes. You must be exhausted.
LILY. ...we can lie down. I want you to take off all these hotel clothes I've got on and I want you to make love with me. And if you'd like to dance first, that's all right. Or if you want to have a drink of whiskey, that's fine too. The only thing you can't do is say no. Don't say anything.
ARCHIE. You don't have to thank me, if that's what you're trying to do. I couldn't just let him die here.
LILY. *(Very firm, and very fast.)* I said you couldn't say anything. You must learn to shut up, Arhie, and you must never ... ever ... assume that you know why anybody is doing anything.
ARCHIE. *(Gets the message.)* I said I would do whatever you wanted and I meant that.
LILY. *(Now much more personal.)* I don't know what's going to happen in the morning. He could wake up mean and kill us both. Or he could take off for Bolivia or just disappear for another ten years. Then again, he might take you up on your offer and marry me. So, this is just a little waiting time before we know what *is* going to happen. It's free clear time. We might as well be all alone in the whole world. And whatever happens in the morning, I won't be seeing you very often, and you are the first person I have genuinely liked in a long time. And if you start threshing wheat, I'll end up helping you, and it'll kill me. This way, unless I've forgotten what to do, which is possible, because it's been ten years I've spent waiting for that man, we're both going to feel a lot better. Now, take my head in your hands and kiss me. *(Her speech has affected a considerable change in Archie. He seems taller, more poised.)*

ARCHIE. *(After the kiss.)* Dancing, or drinking first ... would just waste our time, don't you think?

LILY. You're going to do just fine.

ARCHIE. You are the most beautiful woman I have ever seen.

LILY. You're catching on real fast, Archie. I knew you would.

ARCHIE. I even have one of Mother's quilts.

LILY. Sh-h-h. *(And Lily smiles and a single light remains on the sleeping Outlaw as Archie and Lily step into the cookshack. And there is a change in the lighting as we go from night to dawn. Lights come back up as Archie and Lily walk out of the cookshack, Archie carrying a coffeepot. Lily is wrapped in a quilt, and carries a skillet and some eggs. They walk to the fire and sit sometime during Archie's answer here.)*

ARCHIE. I guess it would be an engineer. The railroad ... I don't know, it's important to me. I could sit there all day, swapping stories with the fireman, check my pressure gauge, watch the sky cloud up, look out back at where we've been, see our smoke ... Chief Engineer on the Overland Flyer. What a job. *(Pauses.)* Or the war could need me, I guess.

LILY. The war would've had you already if they'd elected that Teddy Roosevelt.

ARCHIE. My Dad says President Wilson is just plain yellow. Wouldn't last two weeks as Sheriff of Clovis.

LILY. I'd like to see New York.

ARCHIE. Me too. Know what they've got there? Crowds. *(She laughs.)* I want to bump into things, people, cars ... I don't even know what things. I don't know what I'm talking about. Do you believe there's airplanes?

LILY. *(Laughs.)* Oh, Archie. This is going to make you so mad. I've seen one!

ARCHIE. You have not! You saw a picture of one. I've seen a picture of one. I want to see one fly over my head. Would you ride in one?

LILY. Three years ago, I took the train to St. Louis. It's as far east as I've been. That Teddy Roosevelt was up in an airplane with somebody called the Wright Brothers Flying Team. We were all

down there watching him. He was waving to us. We were waving at him. He got so excited waving he almost fell out of the plane! Oh, it was the best day. People were standing around saying things like take-off and airpocket. *(Her excitement is unlike anything we've seen from her to this point.)*
ARCHIE. Why didn't you tell me this before?
LILY. It's the only story I know. I was saving it for you.
ARCHIE. It's the best story I ever heard.
LILY. There are plenty more out there. All you have to do is get on the train.
ARCHIE. *(Defensively.)* Things happen here. Things are changing here too. I want to be here when it happens. People like me have to stay here and make it happen.
LILY. When it happens here, Archie, it will be secondhand. But I'm not going to say any more about it. You know what I think. Now, tell me how your brother got his hand eaten by the catfish.
ARCHIE. No, you tell me what else you saw in St. Louis. *(Before Lily can answer, the Outlaw stirs and we see that he is awake. Lily and Archie exchange pleased looks. Much too bright.)* Good morning!
OUTLAW. Hold it right there! *(He is seriously disoriented, and at the sound of Archie's voice, he springs up, then dives back down beside the cookshack and holds the gun on them. Archie protects Lily by moving in front of her.)*
ARCHIE. Easy, buddy. It's just us.
OUTLAW. Buddy?
LILY. It's all right, Tom.
OUTLAW. *(Very grumpy, stands up.)* The hell it is!
ARCHIE. How do you feel?
OUTLAW. Bad.
LILY. We've got the coffee all ready.
ARCHIE. How about some eggs?
OUTLAW. *(He grabs his case.)* I gotta get out of here.
LILY. We can have some coffee first. And I'm hungry.
OUTLAW. Good-bye, Lily. Boy.
ARCHIE. Now, you wait a minute. We walked you around for

hours, just the two of us and it was cold out here and you're heavy, mister. We saved your life last night.

OUTLAW. Yeah, and if I don't get going, that threshing crew will come back and you'll get another chance to save my life. You may not care if your brother is dead, but your crew boss is gonna care that he's a man short today. I already said good-bye. That's all you're gonna get! *(Turns to go.)*

ARCHIE. You're on foot, remember? *(A pause.)* Only way out of here's in that car of hers. *(Then having a little fun.)* If you act nice, though, she might let you drive.

LILY. How many eggs, Tom?

OUTLAW. Just two.

LILY. And bacon?

OUTLAW. I'd rather have peaches. Are there any peaches?

LILY. *(Getting up, starting for the cookshack.)* I'll look. Archie?

ARCHIE. I'm not hungry.

OUTLAW. You are too. You should have some eggs. You like peaches?

ARCHIE. *(Setting the frying pan on the fire.)* O.K. Same as him. *(Lily goes into the cookshack. Archie is worried if the Outlaw knows about Lily and him in the cookshack last night. The Outlaw doesn't know anything. As the Outlaw sits down.)* They won't be back before noon. Probably not til six. It's Sunday. Can't miss church. *(The Outlaw nods.)* Do you remember what you said last night?

OUTLAW. I didn't say a thing.

ARCHIE. You asked Lily to marry you. She said yes.

OUTLAW. Out of my head, I guess.

ARCHIE. *(Angry now.)* And you asked me to look in your case, there. *(This disturbs the Outlaw.)*

OUTLAW. *(Firm, hostile.)* Nobody looks in my case. *(Lily comes out with the can of peaches and some bowls, which she hands to Archie.)*

LILY. *(Starting to cook the eggs.)* Now, it won't be but just a minute.

OUTLAW. *(Brightly.)* So, got away again, did I?

LILY. You had help.

OUTLAW. I guess I should thank you.

ARCHIE. *(Angry.)* I wondered when you'd get around to that.

OUTLAW. You didn't have to do it, so I don't have to thank you. You think you always know the right thing to do, boy, well you don't. Maybe I was ready for it. Maybe if you knew about anything besides egg hunts, you'd have let me die. I mean, what do you know about anything, Archie?

ARCHIE. It was Henry told you about the egg hunts. And Henry's dead. I know about *that*.

LILY. *(Insisting that they both calm down.)* We'll just eat out of the skillet, here. *(She hands them each a fork and we have a moment of peace.)*

OUTLAW. *(As they begin to eat.)* I love eggs. Thing I don't understand is how something so good can come from a chicken. A chicken!

ARCHIE. *(Matter of fact.)* I like fried chicken.

OUTLAW. Me too. With biscuits and gravy.

LILY. There are chickens on the farm.

ARCHIE. Her farm. Remember about her farm? Where you're going to live with her?

OUTLAW. Can't stand 'em. Make me nervous. Dirty animals. Shouldn't even be called animals.

ARCHIE. They're not. They're birds.

OUTLAW. They're ugly. They can't even fly.

ARCHIE. They lay eggs for you. They die to make your fried chicken.

OUTLAW. I couldn't live with chickens and that's the end of it.

ARCHIE. Cattle?

OUTLAW. Cattle are dumb.

ARCHIE. Crops?

OUTLAW. Work.

LILY. Just horses then. The horses on the farm are...

OUTLAW. Have to be young to work horses.

LILY. There are young people for hire.

OUTLAW. I don't like young people either. Jumpy. I don't like any of it. I only like eggs.

LILY. No chickens. I promise.

OUTLAW. No. No nuthin'. No marriage. No farm. No nuthin'. *(And there is a terrible pause, while everybody understands what has just been said.)*

ARCHIE. You are so dumb. Nobody cares about outlaws any more. You should've killed me, instead of Henry. He was your last real admirer and you shot him.

LILY. *(Trying to be calm.)* How are we going to wash these dishes?

ARCHIE. *(Bitter, hostile.)* Leave 'em. They'll figure it out! A new grave and dirty dishes. Somebody came in here, killed Henry and ate breakfast.

OUTLAW. They're gonna think you killed him! How about that! After we leave, there's gonna be one gun with one shot fired and one dead man with one bullet in him ... and you. Dammit all, you're gonna get the credit for my good shot.

ARCHIE. You killed my brother and I saved your life!

OUTLAW. And I wouldn't tell anybody if I were you.

ARCHIE. *(Defensive.)* They'll understand. It was the exact right thing to do.

OUTLAW. It's as wrong as it can be, boy. It's one of your new ideas and it's nothin' but trouble. You wait and see.

ARCHIE. That's ridiculous.

OUTLAW. If you had an inch of guts you'd kill me back, and that's what they're all gonna say, the crew, your Dad, all of 'em! Aren't they. I can hear 'em now. "So what'd you do, Archie?" "You did what, Archie?" That's exactly what they'll say. Isn't it!

ARCHIE. I don't know what they'll say.

OUTLAW. You do too. It's exactly what they'll say!

ARCHIE. What if it is? That doesn't make it right. It only means they're as backward as you and Henry.

OUTLAW. No, boy. You should've shot me. You have to kill 'em while you got the chance, or else you'll just have to fight 'em again some other day.

ARCHIE. Well I don't believe that.

OUTLAW. Well I'm glad I'm not gonna be there for the future then. This ain't something Jesse James made up, boy. This is how things are ... here.

ARCHIE. *(Very strong.)* Were ... here.

OUTLAW. *(Stronger still.)* Are! Everywhere!

ARCHIE. No! Not anymore. Not everywhere! No! Just out here in this damn scrub country. We're so far away from everything, everybody acts like there's no rules at all, and anybody can just do whatever they like, well they can't. Or if they can, I don't have to sit here and watch them, not anymore. I've got my own ideas about how people should live and this ain't it. No sir.

OUTLAW. I shot the wrong boy all right. You're scared.

ARCHIE. *(Rejecting both ideas out of hand, suddenly seems very alert, self-possessed, proud.)* I am not. I've got a better idea. *(Picks up the Outlaw's case.)*

OUTLAW. That's mine.

ARCHIE. *(Triumphant, taking charge.)* I'm going to burn them!

OUTLAW. You will not!. You put that down! They're all I've got!

ARCHIE. She's all you've got but you don't know it. Once they're gone, you'll have a chance of finding that out.

OUTLAW. *(Pulls his gun.)* You give them to me!

ARCHIE. *(Crumpling one poster.)* You'll have to kill me for them. I don't think you will. Wouldn't be fair. Actually I like that about you. That and the mint. *(Throwing it in the fire.)*

OUTLAW. *(Archie is right, puts the gun away.)* It won't make any difference. They'll still know who I am.

ARCHIE. Good then. I have your permission. *(Archie opens the case, dumping all the newspaper articles, wanted posters and other bits of evidence of the Outlaw's exploits on the fire. Very formal.)* All the outlaws are dead. McCarty was an outlaw. McCarty must be dead.

LILY. And the only picture we have of him is twenty years old, so who is this old-timer we got here?

ARCHIE. *(Now much more personal.)* You can't just keep riding around. She loves you. You can forget everything that's happened and start all over.

OUTLAW. If I forget everything that's happened, then what do I have that she would want, boy?

ARCHIE. How should I know? But she said she would marry you so there must be something.

OUTLAW. *(To Lily.)* Look, I was pretty groggy last night. I don't remember any of this.

LILY. That's what I said all right.

OUTLAW. Boy I sure don't know why.

ARCHIE. Maybe she likes your talk. *(Pauses a moment.)* Come on. Do you ever know why anybody does anything?

LILY. I also said it better be today or I never want to see you again. *(And there is another pause, but this one is much more pleasant. This one has some acceptance in it.)*

OUTLAW. *(Looking at Lily, but talking to Archie.)* Go ahead. Burn the case, too, why don't you?

ARCHIE. *(Handing it out to him.)* That'd be wasteful. Nice case.

OUTLAW. *(Looks at Lily, then at Archie.)* Keep it.

ARCHIE. *(Dusting it off, looking at it.)* Thanks. I will. I'm gonna need something like this. *(To Lily.)* Do me a favor.

LILY. I owe you one.

ARCHIE. Write to my mother. It's Olivia Tucker, Clovis. Tell her to take care of herself. Tell her...

LILY. ...you did what you could. You'll write when you can.

ARCHIE. Yeah. Thanks.

OUTLAW. Running away, huh, Archie? They'll know you did it for sure, now. Gonna go east? Where they do things civilized?

ARCHIE. I don't know where I'm going. I'm just getting on the train. There's just got to be some town that makes some sense.

OUTLAW. Go east. You'll fit right in.

ARCHIE. Prissy little boy like me.

OUTLAW. Exactly. *(And Archie heads for the cookshack to gather up his things.)*

ARCHIE. *(As he steps up into the cookshack.)* He needs a bath.

OUTLAW. The hell I do!

LILY. I'll see that he gets it. *(As Archie is inside the cookshack, Lily and the Outlaw try to talk again.)* It was the car, wasn't it. If I had come on a horse, none of this would have happened. You just didn't want to ride away in an automobile.

OUTLAW. Just seemed awful fancy, that's all.

LILY. That didn't used to be a problem for you.

OUTLAW. I liked a fancy girl, all right. I sure did.

LILY. Well, then...

OUTLAW. I'm gonna need a new coat. Long, gold color.

LILY. I think we can handle that. *(And he stands there a moment, just looking at her.)*

OUTLAW. Now just how, exactly, are you gonna "see" that I get my bath?

LILY. Oh I'll draw the water, hand you the brush, get myself a beer, pull up a chair and watch. You remember.

OUTLAW. Yeah, it's all comin' back to me now.

LILY. But we'll have to call you something else in town. Tom McCarty is dead.

OUTLAW. It won't work. Roy Luther will know it's me.

LILY. He'll call you whatever you want. He'll call you Clara Mae if you buy him a beer.

OUTLAW. I could be Doc. How about Doc. I was courtin a Doc's daughter so they called me Doc. It's a joke.

LILY. Doc is good.

OUTLAW. Doc it is. *(And now Archie comes out of the cookshack carrying his things, one of which must be his mother's quilt all rolled up.)*

LILY. *(Walking over to him, kissing him.)* Good-bye, Archie.

ARCHIE. I'll send you picture postcards, so don't sell the hotel or move or anything.

LILY. Send me one from France.

ARCHIE. From the war if I get there.

LILY. From France. From New York. From France.

ARCHIE. *(As the Outlaw takes her arm.)* You bet I will. Good-bye, Lily.

OUTLAW. Come on, girl. *(Practically dragging her now.)* A war is just what you need, runt.

ARCHIE. The name's Archie.

OUTLAW. That's a runt name, for sure. Come *on*, girl. *(Walks offstage.)*

LILY. *(Backing away toward the Outlaw.)* Goodness and mercy. *(In farewell.)*

ARCHIE. Huh?

LILY. *(A blessing.)* ...follow you all the days of your life.

ARCHIE. *(Affectionately.)* Oh yeah. What do you think the chances of that are?

LILY. I don't know. Fair.

ARCHIE. Good-bye, Lily.

LILY. *(As she turns to join the Outlaw.)* Let's get out of here. They could be back any time. It's almost noon. *(Archie watches her go, then walks up to Henry's grave and then takes a look around the camp area, wanting to remember what it all looked like. Finally, he seems ready to go, and then remembers what he should do now.)*

ARCHIE. Jesus God in Heaven, it's Archie Tucker from Clovis, New Mexico. And I know you can see me, so you must've seen everything that went on down here tonight and listen, I want to know ... *(Very flip and irritated.)* Was this all your idea? *(Pauses.)* Because if it was ... go work on somebody else for a while. I've got things to do. *(Starts to walk off, then stops, as we hear.)*

LILY. *(From offstage.)* Well, what are you waiting for? Get in. The handle's right there on the door.

OUTLAW. *(From offstage.)* Just getting the feel of her, that's all. Real smooth, isn't she.

LILY. *(From offstage.)* Real shiny too. Wait til it's light. You'll see. *(And as we hear the car doors slam, Archie has something else to say to God.)*

ARCHIE. Well, O.K. I do appreciate what you did for me with that coyote back on the road there, so I'm grateful. Thank you. I mean, I do want to stay in touch. *(He pauses, knowing he won't be in touch as often as he has been in the past, but is excited about what lies ahead for him. We hear the car's engine start, then drive off.)* Tell you what. First time I get up in one of those airplanes. You keep your eye on ol' Archie Tucker. I'll ... *(Raises his hand in a fond salute and smiles.)* ... wave to you. *(The lights, which by now are down to a single light on Archie's face, black out, as the sound of a train whistle and the faint strains of some World War I song end the play.)*

THE END

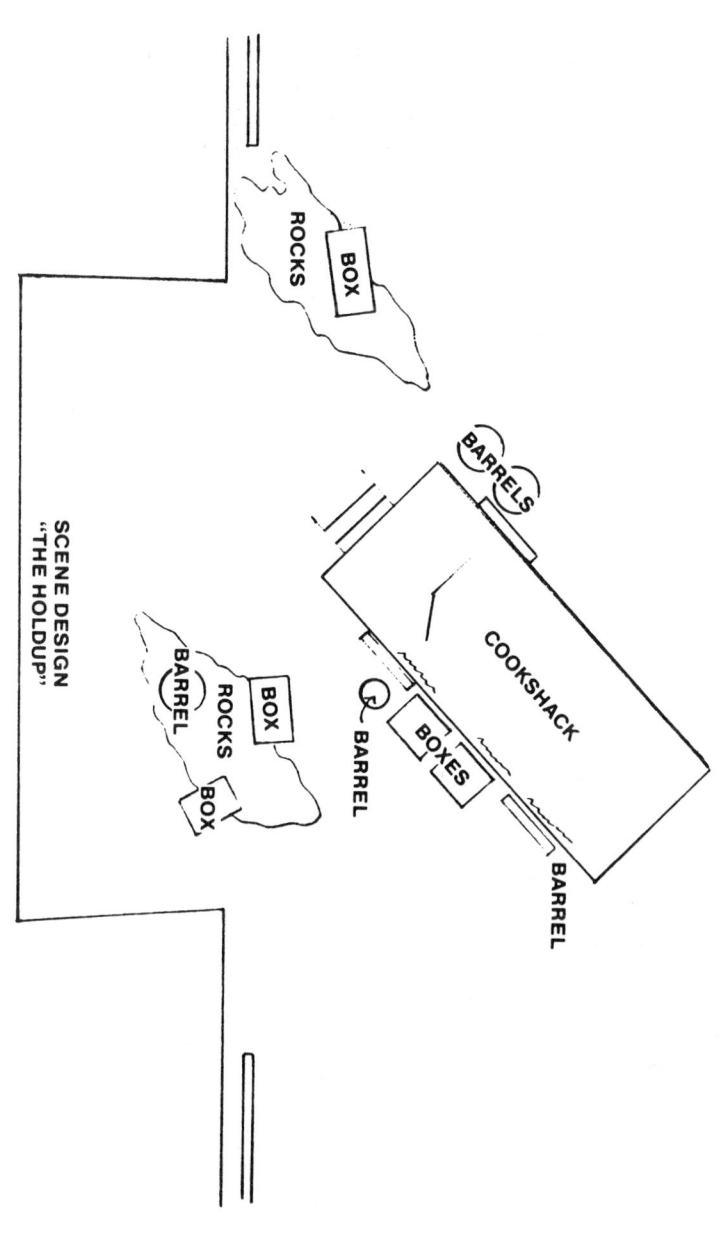

PROPERTY LIST

PRESHOW SETUP

ON PORCH OF COOKSHACK
Chair with
  Cushion
Rope (coiled on nail U of door)
Small wood box with (U of chair, against cookshack)
  Wheat & dressing
Lantern (plugged in)
(2) Nails for Archie's coat and hat
Burlap bag (on D wheel)
(2) Dishtowels (hung on spokes of wheel)

UNDER PORCH OF COOKSHACK
Woodpile

UPSTAGE OF COOKSHACK
Shovel (leans against support L end of cookshack)
Outlaw's hat (set on box)
Brush (set on box)
Mirror
Barrel 1 (large—against UR wheel)
Barrel 2 (medium—against barrel 1)
(2) Ground brush pallets

ON STAGE RIGHT
Bale of hay with
  Speaker plugged in
Ground pallet which hay is set on

DOWNSTAGE OF COOKSHACK
Dressing
  Washtub
  Short pitchfork

Fork of pitchfork
Coil of rope (nylon—used to tie up Archie)
Another washtub
Long pitchfork
Keg
Small box with
    Bucket
Larger box
Barrel with (with handle for easy striking)
    Basin with
        Water
    Enamel cup on rope
    Lid on rope hinge and rope handle on top

INSIDE COOKSHACK
Table with
    Blood pack
    Henry's pistol with
        (2) 22 blank cartridges at 10 and 11 o'clock
    Pie plate with
        Cottage cheese (scrambled eggs)
        Fork
    Pie plate with
        (6) Fake sunnyside up eggs
        Fork
    Whiskey bottle with
        Water
        Cork
    Trivet (for hot frying pan)
    Container of salt
    Unopened can of tomatoes
    Opened can of tomatoes with
        Tomatoes—1 small can chopped in blender & water; can should be ¾+ full
    Black enamel cup
    Pottery bowl with

(5) fresh eggs in shells
　　　Pork
　　Light on table
　Bench with
　　　Quilt (folded in a triangle—point hangs D)
　Chair with
　　　Henry's jacket
　　　Henry's hat
　　　Henry's belt
　　　Henry's scarf
　　　Henry's boots
　Nail with
　　　Belt for quilt on last notch
　Dressing
　Smoke

COOKFIRE PALLET
Pallet (set in U position)
U crate box
L crate box
Cook kettle with
　　Screen
　　Smoke holder
　　Firelights
Coffee pot with
　　Hot coffee ⅓ full
　　Pot holder rag
Black enamel mug (set with coffee pot)

Dirt, raffia & grass all over stage

OFF STAGE RIGHT
Outlaw's pistol
(2) Theatrical blank cartridges and (1) weighted spent
　　cartridge
Sheath with

Hunting knife
Small envelope with (flap torn off)
　　¾ in. baking soda
(3) Sprigs of fresh green mint in water
(2) Slices of beef jerky (Henry)
Car with
　　Lights
　　Cable
　　Track
　　Goggles in glove compartment
Henry's grave

OFF STAGE LEFT

Saddle with (set in first wing onstage of case)
　　Horseblanket
Outlaw's case with (starting on the bottom)
　　Wanted posters
　　Clippings
　　Pamphlet
　　Rolled bundles tied with leather
　　Bundles of clippings stapled
　　Outlaw's photo

OUTLAW'S DRESSING ROOM

Pocket watch and chain
Holster and bullets
Mint
Morphine

LILY'S DRESSING ROOM

Perfume vial and hanky in her purse
Goggles

TODAY'S HOTTEST NEW PLAYS

❑ **MOLLY SWEENEY by Brian Friel, Tony Award-Winning Author of *Dancing at Lughnasa*.** Told in the form of monologues by three related characters, *Molly Sweeney* is mellifluous, Irish storytelling at its dramatic best. Blind since birth, Molly recounts the effects of an eye operation that was intended to restore her sight but which has unexpected and tragic consequences. *"Brian Friel has been recognized as Ireland's greatest living playwright. Molly Sweeney confirms that Mr. Friel still writes like a dream. Rich with rapturous poetry and the music of rising and falling emotions...Rarely has Mr. Friel written with such intoxicating specificity about scents, colors and contours."* - New York Times. [2M, 1W]

❑ **SWINGING ON A STAR (The Johnny Burke Musical) by Michael Leeds. 1996 Tony Award Nominee for Best Musical.** The fabulous songs of Johnny Burke are perfectly represented here in a series of scenes jumping from a 1920s Chicago speakeasy to a World War II USO Show and on through the romantic high jinks of the Bob Hope/Bing Crosby "Road Movies." Musical numbers include such favorites as "Pennies from Heaven," "Misty," "Ain't It a Shame About Mame," "Like Someone in Love," and, of course, the Academy Award winning title song, "Swinging on a Star." *"A WINNER. YOU'LL HAVE A BALL!"* - New York Post. *"A dazzling, toe-tapping, finger-snapping delight!"* - ABC Radio Network. *"Johnny Burke wrote his songs with moonbeams!"* - New York Times. [3M, 4W]

❑ **THE MONOGAMIST by Christopher Kyle.** Infidelity and mid-life anxiety force a forty-something poet to reevaluate his 60s values in a late 80s world. *"THE BEST COMEDY OF THE SEASON. Trenchant, dark and jagged. Newcomer Christopher Kyle is a playwright whose social satire comes with a nasty, ripping edge - Molière by way of Joe Orton."* - Variety. *"By far the most stimulating playwright I've encountered in many a buffaloed moon."* - New York Magazine. *"Smart, funny, articulate and wisely touched with rue...the script radiates a bright, bold energy."* - The Village Voice. [2M, 3W]

❑ **DURANG/DURANG by Christopher Durang.** These cutting parodies of *The Glass Menagerie* and *A Lie of the Mind*, along with the other short plays in the collection, prove once and for all that Christopher Durang is our theater's unequivocal master of outrageous comedy. *"The fine art of parody has returned to theater in a production you can sink your teeth and mind into, while also laughing like an idiot."* - New York Times. *"If you need a break from serious drama, the place to go is Christopher Durang's silly, funny, over-the-top sketches."* - TheatreWeek. [3M, 4W, flexible casting]

DRAMATISTS PLAY SERVICE, INC.
440 Park Avenue South, New York, New York 10016 212-683-8960 Fax 212-213-1539

TODAY'S HOTTEST NEW PLAYS

❏ **THREE VIEWINGS by Jeffrey Hatcher.** Three comic-dramatic monologues, set in a midwestern funeral parlor, interweave as they explore the ways we grieve, remember, and move on. *"Finally, what we have been waiting for: a new, true, idiosyncratic voice in the theater. And don't tell me you hate monologues; you can't hate them more than I do. But these are much more: windows into the deep of each speaker's fascinating, paradoxical, unique soul, and windows out into a gallery of surrounding people, into hilarious and horrific coincidences and conjunctions, into the whole dirty but irresistible business of living in this damnable but spellbinding place we presume to call the world."* - New York Magazine. [1M, 2W]

❏ **HAVING OUR SAY by Emily Mann.** The Delany Sisters' Bestselling Memoir is now one of Broadway's Best-Loved Plays! Having lived over one hundred years apiece, Bessie and Sadie Delany have plenty to say, and their story is not simply African-American history or women's history...it is our history as a nation. *"The most provocative and entertaining family play to reach Broadway in a long time."* - New York Times. *"Fascinating, marvelous, moving and forceful."* - Associated Press. [2W]

❏ **THE YOUNG MAN FROM ATLANTA Winner of the 1995 Pulitzer Prize. by Horton Foote.** An older couple attempts to recover from the suicide death of their only son, but the menacing truth of why he died, and what a certain Young Man from Atlanta had to do with it, keeps them from the peace they so desperately need. *"Foote ladles on character and period nuances with a density unparalleled in any living playwright."* - NY Newsday. [5M, 4W]

❏ **SIMPATICO by Sam Shepard.** Years ago, two men organized a horse racing scam. Now, years later, the plot backfires against the ringleader when his partner decides to come out of hiding. *"Mr. Shepard writing at his distinctive, savage best."* - New York Times. [3M, 3W]

❏ **MOONLIGHT by Harold Pinter.** The love-hate relationship between a dying man and his family is the subject of Harold Pinter's first full-length play since *Betrayal*. *"Pinter works the language as a master pianist works the keyboard."* - New York Post. [4M, 2W, 1G]

❏ **SYLVIA by A.R. Gurney.** This romantic comedy, the funniest to come along in years, tells the story of a twenty-two year old marriage on the rocks, and of Sylvia, the dog who turns it all around. *"A delicious and dizzy new comedy."* - New York Times. *"FETCHING! I hope it runs longer than Cats!"* - New York Daily News. [2M, 2W]

DRAMATISTS PLAY SERVICE, INC.
440 Park Avenue South, New York, New York 10016 212-683-8960 Fax 212-213-1539